Coventry's Countryside

I've savoured England's finest green,
Our National Parks my soul has seen,
Hailed heavens heights, danced Dove dipped dales,
Cast flighted flies in Welshest Wales,
But lifetime's love, my joy supreme,
Embrace Godiva's country cream,
Where I have hived such honeyed hours,
Gift garlanded with fresh field flowers.

Bill Rogers

A COVENTRY WAY ASSOCIATION

Main Objectives of A Coventry Way Association (ACWA).

To promote A Coventry Way (ACW) for the benefit of the community as a Long Distance Path.

To support local authorities in maintaining ACW with working parties drawn from the 2007 membership.

To organise annually a walk that encourages all grades of recreational walkers (including charity walkers) to get into the countryside around Coventry. The event to include a challenge section that would appeal to athletes as well as competitive walkers.

Encourage the use of public transport to get into the countryside near to Coventry.

To make available a reasonably priced and up to date copy of ACW Guide Booklet and the 21 Circular Walks Booklet.

To raise sufficient funds/support/sponsorship to support re-issuing and updating the two publications noted above.

To introduce people to long distance walking and acquaint them with the three other Long Distance Walks close to Coventry (Centenary Way, Heart of England Way and The Oxford Canal Trail).

Encourage all users to abide by The Countryside Code.

Wherever possible on the Way, encourage and support the local authorities in making the country accessible for people with limited mobility.

For information about membership of ACWA, please visit our web site, 'www.acoventryway.org.uk'. See page 104 for committee members 2007.

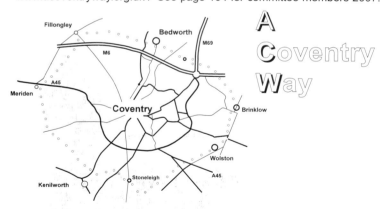

Fred Dowell   1917-2002

It was whilst training with Cyril Bean for the Karrimor Mountain Marathons in the early seventies that the potential of a long distance path around Coventry was discussed. This was realised in 1995 when the first booklet on A Coventry Way was published. For the last 27 years of his life Fred was unable to pursue his many outdoor activities following a terrible accident. However, he continued to encourage the activities of A Coventry Way Association by supporting the annual challenge event and the publication of this booklet. Sadly, Fred died just before this booklet was published.

A Coventry Way Association

Circular Walks

21

by members of
A Coventry Way Association

Circular Walks

by members of A Coventry Way Association.

Contributors:

Design, layout and maps - C J Bean.　　　Collation of history notes - I L Bean.
Wildlife Notes - Ian Tanner (local ecologist).　　Editor - Keith Greenall.
Auditors of walks and other contributors see pages 102/104.
Picture credits see below.

ISBN 0-9526631-2-0　First published 2002.　Revised 2007.　Reprinted 2008.
Published by A Coventry Way Association, 46 Bendictine Road, Coventry CV3 6GY.
Printed by Print5, Coventry.
Reproduced by permission of Ordnance Survey on behalf of the Controller of
Her Majesty's Stationery Office © Crown Copyright 100039609

Permissions
Definitions from *Dictionary of English Place Names* by A. D. Mills (new second edition 1998) by permission of Oxford University Press.
For list of publications used in collating some of the material and contributors from the parishes see page 102.

Sketches by Kevin Wilkins from Iris Bean's photographs.
Other sketches by Maureen Harris & Nicola Bean.
Measured drawing of Coombe Abbey by Mark Hampson.
Front cover, "The old coach road from Berkswell to Coventry", back cover, "Pedlar's Bridge" - Iris Bean
Photograph of Stare Bridge - Duncan Bean.

Every endeavour has been made to obtain permission to use copyright material.
The publishers would appreciate errors or omissions being brought to their attention.

A Coventry Way Association is grateful to the authorities, companies, parish councils and organisations below who have contributed financially to this project

Coventry City Council

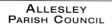

ALLESLEY PARISH COUNCIL

BAGINTON PARISH COUNCIL

BRINKLOW PARISH COUNCIL

CHURCH LAWFORD PARISH COUNCIL

KENILWORTH TOWN COUNCIL

JAGUAR

PEUGEOT

Nuneaton & Bedworth

Warwickshire County Council

Solihull
METROPOLITAN BOROUGH COUNCIL

CONTENTS

Distance Chart *Rounded up or down to nearest 0.5 mile ~ Estimated by Bob Watson*

miles (kilometres)

No	Page	Title	Area of Walks - Start location first	Main Walk	Route A
1	14	Four Greens	Eastern Green, Meriden	7.0 (11.0)	5.5 (9.0)
2	18	Two Greens, A Common & A Well	(Station) Berkswell, Balsall Common	5.5 (9.0)	4.5 (7.5)
3	22	Around Burton Green	Burton Green	7.0 (11.0)	4.5 (7.5)
4	26	The Castle, Common & Manors Beyond	Kenilworth	9.0 (14.0)	8.0 (13.0)
5	30	Town & Country	Coventry, Kenilworth, Stoneleigh, Baginton	12.0 (19.0)	7.0 (11.5)
6	34	After Tea	Stoneleigh, Stareton	3.5 (6.0)	
7	38	As Far As Cubbington	Bubbenhall, Weston u. Wetherley, Cubbington, Stareton	9.0 (14.5)	3.5 (6.0)
8	42	Five Villages	Bub'hall, Stretton, Ryton, Princethorpe, Wappenbury	10.0 (16.0)	8.5 (14.0)
9	46	Dunsmore Heath	Wolston, Ryton on D, Stretton on D	9.0 (14.5)	5.5 (8.5)
10	50	Limestone Trail	Wolston, Ch Lawford, K Newnham, Brinklow, Brandon	8.5 (13.5)	5.5 (9.0)
11	54	The Abbey	Coombe Country Park, Brinklow, Brandon	9.0 (15.0)	6.5 (10.5)
12	58	Eight Bridges	Brinklow, Stretton under Fosse	8.5 (14.0)	7.0 (11.5)
13	62	Withybrook Wander	Withybrook, Ansty, Barnacle, Shilton	7.5 (12.0)	6.0 (10.0)
14	66	Through Bulkington	Ansty, Barnacle, Bulkington, Shilton	8.0 (13.0)	5.5 (9.0)
15	70	The Canal Trail	Hawkesbury Junction, Barnacle, Ansty	8.0 (13.0)	6.0 (9.5)
16	74	Breach Brook Route	Corley Ash, West Bedworth, Keresley	7.5 (12.0)	6.0 (9.5)
17	78	Two Castles & A Manor	Fillongley	5.5 (9.0)	4.0 (7.0)
18	82	Three Corleys	Corley Moor, Corley, Corley Ash	7.5 (12.0)	6.5 (10.5)
19	86	Ancient Arden	Corley Moor, Allesley, Eaves Green	8.0 (13.0)	6.0 (10.0)
20	90	Around The Dome	Meriden, Eaves Green, Kinwalsey	7.5 (12.0)	5.5 (9.0)
21	94	The Broad Ridge	Meriden	4.0 (6.5)	2.5 (4.0)

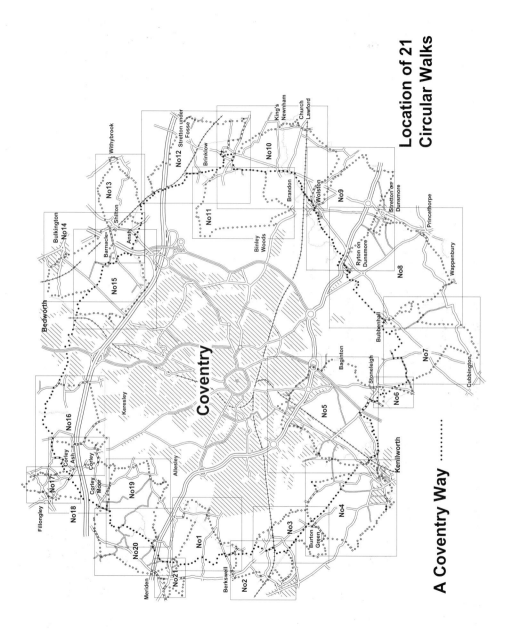

Location of 21
Circular Walks

A Coventry Way ....

Foreword

In the spring of 1995, Cyril Bean published "A Coventry Way". The project had taken over twenty years to bring to fruition. Cyril, a retired Chartered Engineer, used all his professional expertise and his meticulous attention for detail to create a 40 mile circular walk around Coventry that quickly became a favourite long distance path for enthusiastic walkers, and is now included on the latest Ordnance Survey maps.

Having established the "Way", Cyril would have been entitled to sit back and enjoy the plaudits. Fortunately for us, he decided otherwise. Along with members of A Coventry Way Association, he helped to produce this excellent book of 21 circular walks linked to the "Way". You will find all the walks are well researched. Each one has its own potted history, with some intriguing titles, and you will discover places that you did not know existed. The paths in the main have been waymarked, stiles and gates have been put in good order, and farmers and landowners have been consulted where necessary. All they ask is for you to obey The Country Code.

When the Coventry Evening Telegraph published my first book of local country walks in November 1982, the initial print run of 3000 copies sold out in days. Eventually it sold over 20,000 copies. The four that followed are now also out of print, so I very much welcome this book. Let the Association direct you now. Whether it be for a short family stroll or a full days hike, there's plenty to choose from, but may I offer this advice - when you do go out, give yourselves time to stand and stare at the beauty of our local countryside.

Brian Keates
September 2002

Introduction to this Revision

When this book was first published in the Autumn of 2002 Cyril Bean and his fellow contributors never envisaged that the need for a second edition would arrive so soon.

However, people from near and far soon realised what a splendid book had been produced from his original work, establishing the way to enjoy and confidently access the wonderful countryside around Coventry.

Whilst this revised edition attempts to bring the reader up to date with the changes on the 21 walks, the rule which states "Follow The Direction Of The Waymark" has not changed nor have the walks.

Working closely with the local authorities of Warwickshire, Solihull and Coventry, our volunteers have spent many hours improving the walks by replacing stiles with kissing gates to enable walkers with limited mobility to enjoy our local countryside. We continue to clear the paths and improve waymarking and welcome your thoughts on these improvements, whether they be concerning Walk 6 (After Tea) which is now stile free or on the walks which still have much work to be done.

John Green JP
Chairman A Coventry Way Association
March 2007

Objectives

The main objective of this booklet is to encourage walkers to use and discover the countryside near to home. In doing so they will ensure that the paths are brought up to and maintained to a high standard. Also, there is the possibility of using public transport, or at the very least minimising time spent in the car. Without detracting from the more popular walking areas, it is our view that our local countryside is undervalued. The villages and hamlets have plenty to interest the visitor and the area is fortunate in having a significant network of Rights of Way. There should be sufficient to satisfy most classes of walker, with walks of varying distances, none too far from home. However, the note below is important to all who walk in our countryside.

Traffic Notes ⚠

As with all walking guide booklets we are unable to make any risk assessment that would be meaningful. **If you are in doubt at any stage, turn back, do not take any risks**. Exploring the countryside using Rights of Way inevitably results in having to use roads open to traffic, many without pavements. Country lanes are no longer the preserve of local traffic, so be constantly aware. The condition of the verges and adjacent hedges etc. can vary considerably, particularly during the growing season. **GREAT CARE** must be taken on all roads, major or minor, treat them **ALL AS BUSY**. Don't be in a hurry, choose the right crossing point to get a good view of the traffic. There is also a walk where the main and shorter route described in this booklet involves crossing the A45, a dual carriageway. Great care should be taken when crossing this dual carriageway, make sure you look the right way and don't be in a hurry. Please acquaint yourselves with the Pedestrian Rules in the Highway Code, copies of which may be found at libraries or by using the web (www.roads.dft.gov.uk/roadsafety/hc/01.shtml).

Introduction

A Coventry Way, a 40-mile Long Distance Path was first walked in 1974 and a small booklet published in 1995. The background and history are outlined on A Coventry Way Association's web site (www.acoventryway.org.uk).

The 21 circular walks are based on footpaths and bridleways that are linked to A Coventry Way. Individually they offer circular routes from 2.5 miles to 12 miles. For those who wish to walk further than 12 miles, extending them is quite straightforward and some suggestions are given in this booklet. This ensures that all categories of walker can find a distance to suit their needs and the start is only 5 to 7 miles from the centre of Coventry. The best possible way to keep footpaths up to a good standard is to use them. As the local authorities have supported this project, we are sure they will act on any comments that you forward to them. Hopefully, as the Association develops its voluntary group and more people use the paths, improvements will become more noticeable.

The direction notes are detailed and therefore the inevitable changes that take place in our countryside will mean that stiles and gates will replace gaps and vice versa. There is a move by the authorities to gradually replace stiles with kissing gates and this is welcome. It will enable those with limited mobility to take part in this very rewarding activity. Please keep in contact with the Association's website, as this will list any changes that come to our attention.

Twenty routes have short cuts giving the opportunity to either have a good all day trek or alternatively a couple of afternoon strolls. Hopefully using these walks will encourage walkers to take up the very rewarding pastime of long distance walking. The best way to start is near at home on A Coventry Way. You can easily try out your gear, ring home for a lift or request delivery of the tent pole you may have forgotten. The Way and the 21 circular walks share some footpaths with A Heart of England Way, Centenary Way and The Oxford-Coventry Canal Trail.

The layout, a map with adjacent route directions, can be easily carried in a standard map case or plastic bag. There is then no necessity to turn pages, a source of irritation especially if it is wet, cold, and windy. These two pages are preceded with supporting information on various topics, to be read before you start or when you are having lunch. The maps contain enough information to navigate around the route and hopefully will entice the map shy users to get their noses into the excellent Ordnance Survey maps that are readily available in the UK.

Starts

The direction notes are numbered and the position where they begin is shown on the map as No1, along with its grid reference. Although for convention a start is chosen, this doesn't preclude walkers choosing their own preference and beginning at any suitable direction note number. So plan your walk and start in relation to where you want to have lunch or tea, or a long look around a particular village or hamlet.

Map Scales

The scales in this booklet range from 1.5in = 1 mile (1:42 000) to 4.5in = 1 mile (1:14 000). The aim is to have as large a map as possible combined with direction notes on two adjacent A5 pages (i.e map case). It is most unlikely that the average walker will complete more than one walk at a time. Our experience is that you soon get used to the scale in the first couple of fields and our advice is always to pace it out, if you are in doubt.

Wildlife

Each walk has its own wildlife note, prepared by Ian Tanner. His notes can also be of interest if you are attempting the 40-mile Long Distance Path, as the link walks cover most of the 40 miles.

Hedges are a significant part of the English landscape. The maps show the field boundaries adjacent to the walk and the text will say at the time of publication whether it's a hedge or fence. We have seen many hedges removed over the last twenty years or so but on one of these walks there is a long hedge that has been refurbished. A notice, *"This hedge is not being destroyed. It is being coppiced and replanted under the countryside stewardship scheme"*, was positioned for all walkers to see. Well done, it's doing very well. See if you can locate it. If you notice a hedge being removed please contact the County Ecologist on 01926 418060.

Public Transport (see page 101)

Where possible, the bus stops for the starts are shown as a small dot and (bs). Other bus stops are shown in case you need either to use or prefer another start point, or need to cut short a walk. Details of bus numbers are shown on the first page of each walk. As they are subject to occasional changes, please check using the numbers shown on page 101. This also applies to the train times for the two railway stations at Tile Hill and Berkswell.

Field Paths

The cross-field path locations can vary, either formally or informally. The most noticeable changes occur near habitation when a field is planted with young crops. Local dog walkers will initially site the path and walkers will inevitably follow. In these instances the map and directions might vary. Field paths are part of our national heritage, some of them go back to prehistoric times. They are invariably the shortest route from one village to another and by using them we can ensure that they are handed down for posterity as a pleasurable form of recreation and access to the countryside. All of them are steeped in local history and folklore, as the notes on some walks will illustrate. As well as village to village, some were used for children to walk to school and of course their parents to get to work

Choosing suitable footwear

No doubt many of you will have your own preferences. However, for those who need some advice about footwear suitable for walking in our local countryside, we offer the following. If the walk is longer than five or six miles then walking boots or shoes are, most likely, the best option. Some of the walkers who checked out the routes used wellingtons, particularly during the muddy seasons. However, they must be the right size with, as is usual, two pairs of socks, one thin next to the skin and a thicker softer one next to the wellington. This seems to work reasonably well, the theory being that the thin socks stick to your feet and the thick to the wellingtons or boots. Movement is then between the socks and not your precious feet. It may be worth a try, but experiment on very short distances first.

Canal Towpaths

British Waterways are responsible for the condition of the towpaths that are used on some of the walks. They actively encourage walkers and are investing heavily in keeping their paths up to date and any difficulties should be reported directly to them.

Condition of Footpaths/Bridleways

If you find the way is difficult to follow through lack of waymarking, that some of the stiles are in a poor state, or gates are locked etc., we strongly advise that you take the time to register your observations with the local authority. You will find that their expert advice and experience will be used, resources permitting, to improve the situation. Warwickshire County Council will advise on any Right of Way included in this booklet and will indicate the particular authority responsible, if it is not in their area.

Public Houses and Refreshment Outlets

Page 100 lists all the outlets with their telephone numbers. It is important, to avoid disappointment, that you check before you start a walk that the establishment is open and can satisfy your requirements. It is courteous, if you can, to ask permission to park at a public house and this can always be complemented by purchasing refreshments.

Direction Notes

Some of you may wonder why there is so much detail in the direction notes. When routes are well waymarked there is no need to describe the route in such a detailed manner. Unfortunately, waymarks deteriorate or get vandalised so there is a need in difficult locations, or when there are alternatives, to guide the non map reader more clearly. However, during auditing it became difficult to distinguish between easy parts and more difficult ones, hence you will find most of the detail is included. The countryside is always changing and no doubt you will find a pedestrian gate replacing a stile, or a sleeper bridge missing, or sometimes a concrete drive that has been there for many years being replaced by something different. Seasonal changes can lead to masking of waymarks, posts and other objects used to guide the walker. Please tell us either by letter, phone, email or via the communication page on our web site, where we will try and list all the changes that come to our notice.

Information Notes

As Coventry is virtually surrounded by countryside, it follows that there is a large number of contiguous parishes. Some of these have supported this publication with financial contributions and interest notes. Also, it has been pleasing to note the increase in parish support for the Rights of Way over the last few years. The brief interest notes have just scratched the surface. Hopefully, further interest notes and other details can be added by local contributors and walkers when this booklet is re-published in the next few years, so please keep in contact. In the text, DB is a reference to the Domesday Book.

Further Activities

The publication of this booklet will hopefully encourage more people into the countryside that surrounds Coventry and this will inevitably lead to the paths being upgraded to a better standard. The Kenilworth Footpath Preservation Group and Church Lawford Parish Council strive to keep the paths in their area up to a very high standard. We are sure other parishes and organisations are also doing whatever they can to achieve similar results. It would be a significant achievement if our Association could be part of this activity. If you wish to help with maintaining the footpaths described in this booklet and those close by, please make contact with our Association.

Layout of Walk Information:

Basically each walk is described in four companion pages.

First page   : Introduction and brief information/wildlife.
Second page   : Continuation of above.
Third page   : Route description.
Fourth page   : Map.

This allows the route description to be next to the map and can therefore be viewed together in a map case. General information includes public transport, refreshment/public houses, brief notes on history, wildlife and some industrial archaeology.

Diagram of Main Walk and its shorter Route A

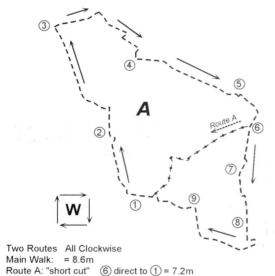

Two Routes   All Clockwise
Main Walk: = 8.6m
Route A: "short cut" ⑥ direct to ① = 7.2m

Where appropriate the **Main Walk** has a short cut giving an **A Route** **The Main Walk** is denoted by a dashed line :- ▬ ▬ ▬ ▬ ▬ ▬
Route A uses a short cut on the Main Walk thus :- ▬•▬•▬•▬•
The letter **A** is positioned on the map to indicate the area covered by Route A. The point at where a short cut can be followed is shown on the map with a broken arrow.

Route A :- ----->

Walkers who want to cover the other part of the Main Walk, ie "B routes" as a separate outing should note they can be followed using the map. The direction note for the short cut is only described in one direction.

Map Symbols

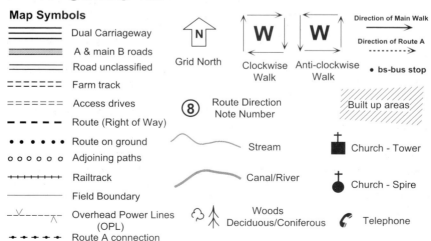

Abbreviations used in Route Directions:

In order to maintain the principle of keeping the map and direction notes as companions, (i.e. to avoid turning the page over) abbreviations have been used. These are only necessary on the routes of 8 miles or so, but they have been used on all the walks, even the shorter ones, so that you get used to them.

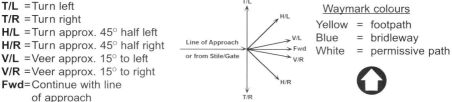

T/L =Turn left
T/R =Turn right
H/L =Turn approx. 45° half left
H/R =Turn approx. 45° half right
V/L =Veer approx. 15° to left
V/R =Veer approx. 15° to right
Fwd=Continue with line
     of approach

Line of Approach
or from Stile/Gate

Waymark colours

Yellow = footpath
Blue = bridleway
White = permissive path

x-stile	=	Over/climb/cross stile	f/g	=	Field gate (tractor width)
k/g	=	Kissing Gate	WMP	=	Waymark Post
p/g	=	Pedestrian/Bridleway Gate	WM	=	Waymark
s/b	=	Sleeper Bridge	PH	=	Public House
bs	=	Bus Stop	OPL	=	Overhead Power Lines
f/b	=	Foot Bridge/handrail	Ch	=	Church

The following are added to the text to confirm that you are walking in the correct direction. But remember, hedges can be removed and fences re-positioned. All the maps show hedges alive and kicking in 2007 (noting that some field boundaries could be fences).

The headland "is the border of a field where the plough turns".

cross-field = Route is not on field boundary.
hg-left = Hedge on your left (on headland).
hg-right = Hedge on your right (on headland).
fc-left = Wire or wooden fence on your left.
fc-right = Wire or wooden fence on your right.
Culvert:- underground stream in piped/brick structure.

Notes to assist in making your walk free of hassle.

Changes are inevitable in the countryside but it is safe to say that not many Rights of Way (ROWs) are extinguished. If the ROW is different to what your OS map or the maps in this booklet indicate there could be a good reason. Stiles become pedestrian or kissing gates etc and farmers, quite rightly, have practical allowances when ploughing and establishing new crops.

If in doubt about the route do not take a confrontational approach, as the farmer/landowner is well aware of his responsibilities and rights. If you need to find out more, or report an obstruction, see page 104 for the appropriate authority.

As far as is possible follow the way-marked route, even if it doesn't match your interpretation of your current OS Map or the maps in this booklet.

Our web site (www.acoventryway.org.uk) will have a section that deals with all the changes that are brought to our attention. Please let us know if you find any.

The need to give precise direction notes may not be obvious during periods when waymarking and pedestrian traffic give a very clear indication of the way ahead. However, during the winter, and when ploughing and crops are being established, the direction to follow may not be so clear.

Start : Junction of Hockley Lane and Eastern Green Lane
Grid Ref. SP 274,803
Direction : Anticlockwise
Main Walk: = 7.0 miles
Route A : = 5.5 miles
OS Maps : (p = part)
: Landranger 140
: Pathfinder 935p
: Pathfinder 955p
: Explorer 221
Refreshments : (page 100
Poacher's Retreat, Eastern Green.
Queen's Head, Meriden.
Bull's Head, Meriden.
Pub. Transport : (page 101
Start 10, 43 & 43A.
On or near route
900 Coventry to Birmingham (Daily service)
192 & 194 Coventry to Solihull (Mon to Sat)
Parking : Carefully in streets adjacent to start.

Brief Information and Outline of Route

These greens were once areas of common land which mainly disappeared under the Enclosures Act. The walk crosses over Pickford Brook & then later joins one of its tributaries out to Meriden. It then follows A Coventry Way (South) until Benton Green, returning thro' Flint's Green back to the start.

Eastern Green: The local church is St Andrew; it had a Victorian vicarage where the Coventry artist James E Kessell had his studio. The present vicarage is a modern house close by.

Pickford Green: The route passes Pickford Grange Farm down to the brook and west to skirt Millison's Wood.

Meriden: Then on to the old Saxon village of "Alspath", now part of Meriden. The village was once owned by Lady Godiva. Past Moat House Farm, part of the moat can still be traced south of its garden but this is in a private residence and not on the Right of Way.

Moat House Farm

Kevin Wilkins

Snippets:-
In the original Coventry Way Booklet we included overhead pylon lines crossing near Blind Hall. Later someone pointed out that we had got them in the wrong place. It needed some digging to find out our apparent error. They were there, now they are gone! A line feeding the West of Coventry had been removed and you can still see a redundant pylon in the field adjacent to Coventry Road and Benton Green Lane. The only thing you can rely on with some certainty are contours.

The church of St Lawrence, probably founded in Saxon times, still has an old horse mounting block by its main entrance. Turn south along the "lost route to Berkswell" and past St Lawrence's Well, now dry.

Berkswell: (See page 18) Eventually, on the outskirts of Berkswell, pass Blind Hall, a timber framed building dating back to Tudor times. The tree lined track towards Hill House (see front cover) is the continuation of Blind Lane, once the coach road to Coventry cutting out the steep hill at Berkswell. Ahead is Hill House, a Grade II listed building, that was built in the 19th century on the site of an older dwelling. Reaching **Benton Green** a small hamlet and then onto **Flint's Green** possibly named after a family called Flint who lived in Berkswell and owned land in this area. From Coventry Road across Back Lane to Eastern Green is now a footpath, but was once an old coaching road called Flint's Lane. This could be a continuation of the Blind Lane coach road.

Wildlife

This part of the Ancient Arden landscape is indicative of the west of Coventry, with some large areas of woodland, numerous ponds, irregular shaped fields and some fine examples of species rich grasslands.

The walk passes between three woodland blocks between sections 2 and 3. Millison's Wood, which is shown on the map, is the largest of the three woods and is managed as a woodland coppice. The wood is largely birch, but boasts an impressive array of woodland plants including bluebell, wood sorrel, enchanter's nightshade, but summer visitors will be most impressed by the show of foxglove, which attracts a large number of nectar seeking bees. The area is managed by Solihull Metropolitan Borough Council and has been designated as a Local Nature Reserve. The other two woodlands are Crow Wood and Spring Wood, both are dominated by birch, although Crow Wood contains some large mature oak trees.

The ponds in the area are as varied as they are numerous. Some are managed almost like garden ponds with lilies and are generally fish stocked. Others are more typical of farm ponds and have shallow banks with emergent vegetation and waterweed. With a move from pastural farming to arable production and the need for high fertilizer applications because of the poor soil quality some ponds have become heavily eutrophic. These ponds often have very little vegetation and become choked with algae each summer. Look out for amphibians from March through to May.

Although species rich grasslands are something of a rarity, grassland species can be seen along road side verges and hedge banks. The churchyard near Moat House Farm offers the weary traveller some insight into what it's all about. By July the delicate blue of harebell can be seen waving in the breeze with the stunning purples of lesser knapweed and deep orange yellows of cat's ear.

Kevin Wilkins

Old sign post and kissing gate leading to Hill House Farm - RIP 2001

Harebell

Main Walk

1. Walk along Eastern Green Lane towards the city for 200m, **T/L** between the middle of four apartment buildings. Thro' k/g & hg-right to go thro' k/g, cross-field to gap & then hg-left to bottom, follow round right, **T/L** over f/b. **Fwd**, pick up hg-left & go up thro' a series of k/gs bearing left until "OPL" at outward hedge corner. Cross-field to pylon, thro' k/g then **H/L** cross-field to field corner. Thro' k/g, hg-left, then down steps to road.

   fwd with hg-right to reach & x-stile in field corner. Hg-right, pool left, **fwd** to field corner, **H/L** in front of another pond to reach hedge, keeping hg-right bear round to the right to another corner. **T/L** to leave "Heart of England Way", **fwd** cross-field on old hedge/fence line to go thro' k/g in opposite hedge. Hg-right, past pond to corner, x-stiles next to gate. **Fwd** down drive to road.

2. **T/L** up road & then **T/R** to next corner. **T/L** down track towards Pickford Grange Fm. Just past farm, thro' f/g, **fwd** then x-stile right of metal gate. Hg-right x-stile left of f/g. Hg-left down towards two f/bs in corner, do not cross. **T/R**, brook on left over next two fields. Thro' k/g and over s/b to continue over next field with initially brook on left, follow hg-left round right until stile is reached near wood, x-stile. (**Route A** see below).

3. Cross-field, initially keep parallel to the boundary of wood on right. **Fwd** leaving the boundary of the wood to aim for the opposite hedge line towards the far right hand corner. As short hedge comes in on left look for & go thro' k/g left of metal gate in this hedgeline. **T/R**, hg-right, continue to end of field. X-stile, **H/R** using a permissive path off to the right that enters Church Lane. **T/L** & follow road around to the right, pass Vicarage Mews on left to just before road turns sharp right.

4. Enter field on left by gap at side of metal gate (WMP) to join ACW. **H/L** towards hedge on left. Keep hg-left, the next stile is just off field corner. Continue with hg-left to cross s/b & stile in corner, **H/L** thro' next field (hedge curving away to left) to x-stile in corner, with hg-left uphill to x-stile next to metal gate. **H/L** uphill across field to go thro' k/g. Keep hg-left then fc-left, thro' paddock & thro' k/g into access track & **fwd** down gravel track to road.

5. **Fwd** over road & x-stile, with hg-left follow farm track & after 150m go thro' hedge gap. **Fwd** with hg-right & at the end of this field, **fwd** thro' hedge gap, pass larger gap on right to continue

6. **T/R** & in a short distance **T/L** & go down Benton Green Lane, continue past lane on right (leaving ACW) to next corner. Just under "OPL" **T/L**, thro' f/g, along hedged/fenced track over concrete s/b, then x-stile, **T/L** & x-stile, **fwd** stream & hedge left. Thro' gap, **H/R** cross-field to far corner. X-stile on left, hg-right until a stile is reached (on your right!), cross to other side of hedge. **T/L**, hg-left to reach & x-stile into fenced path, continue & go thro' garden left of cottage to road.

7. **T/R** along road for 220m, **T/L** thro' gap and in a short distance x-stile on right. Hg-left to x-stile, **fwd** on to concrete drive passing farm on right to road.

8. X-stile opposite & follow track, continue hg-left to s/b & x-stile. **V/R** cross-field to outward hedge corner, right of school. Hg-right to x-stile into enclosed path. **Fwd** to reach road, **H/L** into Church Lane. **T/R** to Finish.

Route A

At the end of Note 2. **T/L**, cross-field to corner with copse on right. X-stiles & s/b, **T/R** for 15m **T/L** up rough track to opposite hedge line. Pick up farm track, hg-left, stay on this track to road. **T/R** for 375m, **T/L**, x-stile, hg-left over two fields. In the next field leave hedge after approx. 50m, **V/R** & aim for stile in hedge/fence between farm enclosure & barns. X-stile, **V/L** cross-yard to join farm drive. **Fwd** down drive to road. Continue with Note 6.

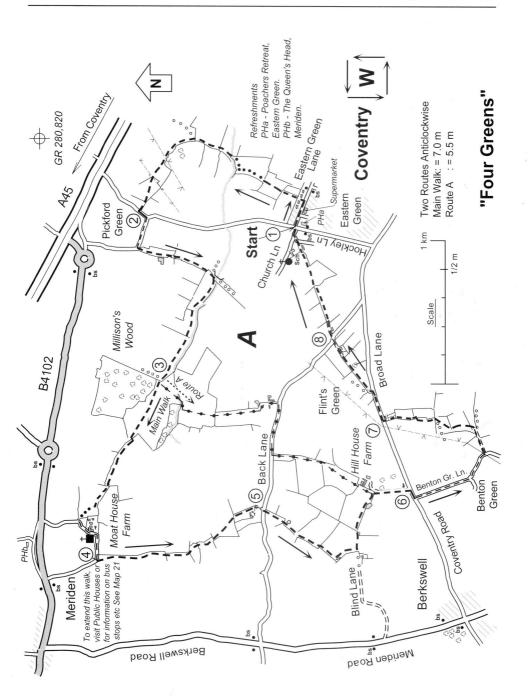

GR 280,820

A45

From Coventry

N

Pickford Green ②

Millison's Wood

Route A ③

Main Walk

B4102

bs

bs

Moat House Farm

Meriden ④

+

PHb

bs

To extend this walk, visit Public Houses or for information on bus stops etc See Map 21

Berkswell Road

Meriden Road

Berkswell

bs

Blind Lane

bs

Back Lane ⑤

Benton Gr. Ln. ⑥

Benton Green

Coventry Road

Hill House Farm ⑦

Flint's Green

Broad Lane

⑧

Start ①

Church Ln

Sch

Hockley Ln

bs

PHa

Eastern Green

Supermarket

bs

Eastern Green Lane

Refreshments
PHa - Poachers Retreat, Eastern Green.
PHb - The Queen's Head, Meriden.

Coventry

W

A

Two Routes Anticlockwise
Main Walk := 7.0 m
Route A   : = 5.5 m

1 km   1/2 m

Scale

"Four Greens"

© Crown Copyright

Start : Berkswell Station
Grid Ref. SP 244,776
or
The Bear Inn, Berkswell
at Note 3
Grid Ref. SP 246,791
Direction : Clockwise
Main Walk: = 5.5 miles
Route A   : = 4.5 miles
OS Maps : (p = part)
*   : Landranger 139p*
*   : Landranger 140p*
*   : Pathfinder 955*
*   : Explorer   221*
Refreshments : (page 100
Bear Inn, Berkswell
Railway Inn,
Berkswell station
Pub. Transport : (page 101
Train to outside Berkswell
(Daily service)
Buses on or near route
192 & 194 (Mon to Sat)
Parking :
Customers of Railway Inn or
station.
Customers of Bear Inn or
careful parking near village
centre.

Snippets:-
Berkswell Museum (at rear of
Almshouses) opening times
2 pm to 6 pm Sundays, Easter
then May to September.
Not too long ago the hand
pump at the crossroads was
quite a feature. After an
accident it was renovated and
returned to its rightful place.
On the village green there is
the Coronation Oak
(June 2nd 1953) surrounded
with its recently refurbished
seat.
The stocks have 5 holes, does
anyone know why?

Brief Information and Outline of Route

From the station and Railway Inn pass through the newly developed fishing ponds. At Note 2 pass the early "Tudor" Ram Hall Farm, home of the famous award winning Berkswell sheep's milk cheese. The building has stone mullion windows and is a Grade II listed building. It once had a moat and it has a priest hole in one of the bedrooms. Then on to **Berkswell** (*Berschewell* in the DB, a spring or stream of a man called Beorcol), with its stocks on the green and a natural spring, Berk's Well, on the way to St John Baptist Church, built in Norman times on a Saxon site. In the churchyard is the war memorial consecrated in 1920 built of local sandstone on the site of the original church school. The old rectory, now The Well House, was a hospital for wounded soldiers during the First World War. Beyond can be seen Berkswell Hall, now converted into modern flats in 1984. The alms-houses facing the green were built in 1853 for twelve aged people from the parish. Back at the crossroads is The Bear Inn or Bear and Ragged Staff as it was formerly known. It dates back to the 15th century and was then part of the Berkswell estate. The inn was the site of the annual hiring fair. It was sold by the estate in 1951. The Bear was the best "real fire" pub in Coventry and Warwickshire for 2002. A carrier service ran twice weekly from Berkswell to Coventry in the 1920s on Tuesdays & Fridays for 6d return.

Simone Whitehurst

Berkswell Village Stores and
Post Office
Officially reopened June 2002.

Berkswell Museum holds a wide ranging collection of domestic, agricultural and other exhibits, all relating to the parish and housed in a listed 16th century timber framed cottage, situated to the rear of the alms-houses in the centre of the village. The collection features information and artifacts relating to Maud Watson, the Rector's daughter, who was the first female tennis champion at Wimbledon in 1884. Maud and her sister Lilian played each other in the first final, thus beating the Williams sisters by well over 100 years. Another celebrity featured at the museum is Bob Wyatt, a former England cricket captain, who lived in the parish as a boy and played for the village team. The cannon on the lawn in front of the Museum, along with a magnificent shield which is housed inside the building (look for the double-headed eagle), was captured during the Crimean War by Sir Eardley-Wilmot, Lord of the Manor in the mid 1850s.

Now at the Coventry Road, before following the footpath on the right, you can walk on a few yards to visit Berkswell animal pound. Through **Benton Green** and then **Carol Green**, at the junction with Truggist Lane pass Tower House, called by locals "Cow Pen Castle". Apparently a previous occupier had been the keeper of the local animal pound. Cross the Kenilworth-Berkswell Greenway to "Old" Waste Lane in **Balsall Common** (*Beleshale* in 1185, nook of land of a man called Baell(i)). Just off route on the main road is Windmill Lane where the fully restored Berkswell Windmill can be seen, built in the early 19th century on the site of an earlier post mill. Back to Waste Lane and across fields to **Berkswell** station.

Simone Whitehurst

Berkswell Windmill

Foxglove

Wildlife

Whilst wandering along Waste Lane it is worth noting the old orchard on your left. Small orchards such as this used to be common place and now, as with this one, have become neglected, prone to disease or destruction. This particular orchard contains pear, plum, damson etc. and may include some old varieties of fruit tree.

On leaving Waste Lane you pass through an area of rich grassland containing a spring. The drier areas include species such as betony, lesser knapweed, tufted vetch, tormentil, lesser stitchwort, pignut, bird's foot trefoil with bluebell and foxglove occurring on the northern field boundary. The wet areas contain rushes, sedges, wetland grasses and redshank, particularly rich in invertebrates.

Main Walk

1. Starting from the Station, **T/R** just past The Railway Inn and follow short unmade road, **T/R** into path to field opposite bungalow (441). **T/L**, fc-left to x-stile, with railway on right **fwd** up to bridge, **T/R** over railway. **Fwd** between pools to x-stile, **fwd** cross-field to x-stile, f/b near stream junction. **H/R**, stream right to road. **T/L** up road for 15m and x-stile on right, hg-left until nearing stream junction x-stile ahead. Over s/b (ignore s/b on right) **T/L**, initially hg-left, then **fwd** cross-field to x-stile onto road.

2. Cross road and **fwd** along lane towards Ram Hall. At the Hall x-stile on right, fence then farm left to x-stile by gate in left-hand corner. Hg-right to x-stile in corner. **T/R**, hg-right round corner up to field corner. X-stile on right, **T/L**, hg-left over three fields to reach road via access alongside bungalow (Berkswell Village). **T/R** to crossroads.

3. **Fwd** up Coventry Road, **T/R**, just past Pound Close into small track to go thro' k/g. **Fwd** cross-field (large) to x-stile in hedge opposite. Over track to gap opposite, **V/L** thro' two fields to reach a stile at the end of a lane. Do not cross stile, **T/R**, hg-left to go round to outer field corner (Sign Post). Cross-field, aim to reach an outer field corner just left of pylon, **fwd** hg-right to x-stile in corner. **T/L**, hg-left x-stile in field corner. **T/L**, hg-left over two fields, go thro' gap using long s/b and with hedge veering away to left, continue to stile opposite. Do not cross stile, **T/R**, hg-left to x-stile & s/b, **fwd** hedge near left to s/b & x-stile. **Fwd** cross-field over footbridge/stile, cross-field, to pick up and keep house fence left, thro' k/g, x-stile onto road.

4. **T/L** and then shortly **T/R** along Truggist Lane, **T/L** into Hodgett's Lane. **Fwd** along road, over railway bridge, immediately **T/R** down access road. **Fwd** for approx. 200m to go thro' p/g on left, just past detached house. **H/R** over track & go thro' p/g in ranch fence to x-stile in far corner. **T/L** along gravel drive for 50m, **V/L** to x-stile a short distance in front. Hg-right, round under OPL to x-stile. Hg-right, bear round right, thro' hedge gap, over s/b, short field to x-stile up steps to the Greenway. (**Route A** see below).

5. **Fwd** over Greenway & down embankment opposite, x-stile, hg-right over three fields, to exit x-stile, onto track and **fwd** to road. **T/R** along road (Old Waste Lane). As road turns left (to main road) carry straight on, x-stile on left of row of cottages. Hg-right, x-stile and s/b. **Fwd,** nursery boundary left, fc-right. **T/L** at field boundary ahead and in 30m x-stile on right, **fwd** initially hedge on left, over three fields keeping the same line to x-stile just off field corner. **Fwd** along track/road to reach Barratt's Lane. Continue **fwd** and immediately after Pool Orchard x-stile on right. Hg-right over two fields, then hg-left to x-stile in corner, **T/L** (ignore p/g), keep hg-left or near left over four fields to go thro' k/g onto road.

Route A

At the end of Note 4. **T/R** along Greenway, for approx. 1km. At the end of the Greenway **T/L** down bank and x-stile into walkway, x-stile & s/b into field. **H/R** cross-field to stile in corner to join main route. **Fwd** hg-left or near left over three fields to go thro' k/g onto road.

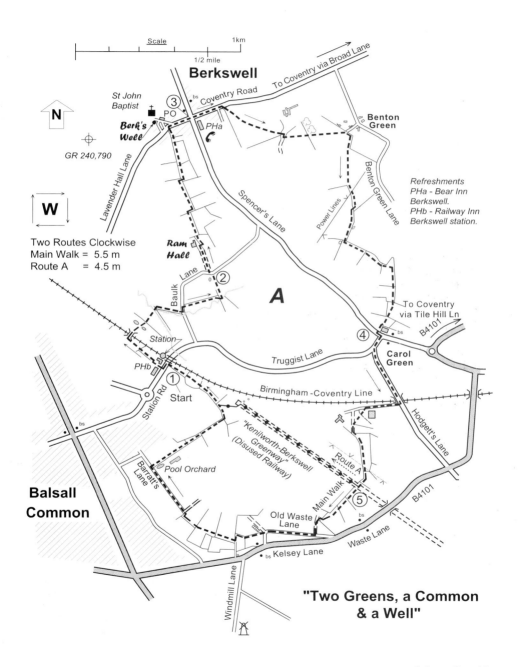

Berkswell

Scale 1km
1/2 mile

St John Baptist
Berk's Well
GR 240,790

N

W

Two Routes Clockwise
Main Walk = 5.5 m
Route A   = 4.5 m

To Coventry via Broad Lane

Coventry Road

PO

PHa

Benton Green

Spencer's Lane

Power Lines

Benton Green Lane

Lavender Hall Lane

Refreshments
PHa - Bear Inn
Berkswell.
PHb - Railway Inn
Berkswell station.

Ram Hall

Baulk Lane

②

A

To Coventry via Tile Hill Ln

④

B4101

Carol Green

Station

PHb

①
Start

Station Rd

Truggist Lane

Birmingham -Coventry Line

Hodgett's Lane

Balsall Common

Barratt's Lane

Pool Orchard

"Kenilworth-Berkswell Greenway" (Disused Railway)

Route A

Main Walk

⑤

Old Waste Lane

Waste Lane

B4101

Kelsey Lane

Windmill Lane

"Two Greens, a Common & a Well"

© Crown Copyright

1/5/10

Start : The Peeping Tom Cromwell Lane see Parking and Snippets below
Grid Ref. SP 272,766
Direction : Clockwise
Main Walk: = 7.0 miles
Route A : = 4.5 miles
OS Maps : Landranger 140
: Pathfinder 955
: Explorer 221
Refreshments : ℓ page 100
The Peeping Tom
Burton Green
Pub. Transport : ℓ page 101
Train to Tile Hill Station
Buses
Start and on or near route 192, 194 & 81E.
Parking : Public House customers, please ask permission.

Snippets:-
If starting from Tile Hill railway station, turn right on exit and continue on right pavement until reaching the junction with Westwood Heath Rd. Cross to the opposite side at a safe point and after 200m turn into walkway on your left (Note 1 page 24).

Beanit Farm had an unexploded bomb or shell from the November 9th 1940 air raid on Coventry found on its land.

The Coventry Eagle Cycle and Motor Co. Ltd. address was Duggins Lane, Tile Hill, Coventry, listed in the 1950 Manufacturers Directory for Coventry.

Route A may look as though it is going in the wrong direction for a short cut. To keep to the ROW you must use the bridge over the Greenway.

Brief Information and Outline of Route

Starting at The Peeping Tom, **Burton Green** (Burton usually old English *Burh-tun*, a fortified farmstead), which was originally a cottage issued with a licence to sell drinks to the men building the railways each end of Cromwell Lane. The lane takes its name from the troops which stayed in the area on their way to the siege at Kenilworth Castle. Cromwell himself is reputed to have stayed in Cromwell Cottage, situated towards Tile Hill Station. An animal pound can be seen by the railway bridge in Cromwell Lane. The pound is on an old cattle drove road from the Welsh hills to London.

Pass Burton Green Farm with an inscription carved in stone on its gable end.
Further along Hob Lane is the local school which is still open and thriving.

JOHN CR ANMORE 1829

Over the field past Moat Farm, built in Tudor times.

Black & White Tudor buildings

Kevin Wilkins

Then North to Beanit Farm, past the sub-station along Kenilworth-Berkswell Greenway, once the old LNWR line built in 1848 and closed in 1969.

Along to Hodgett's Lane and a good view of Beechwood Tunnel back via Benton Green Lane to Reeves Green noting the site of the old Eagle Cycle Factory on the left before Duggins Lane. The lane is named after the Duggins family of blacksmiths who have worked here for many years.

Over the railway skirting round the back of Nailcote Hall. The house dates from the 16th century, but was enlarged in the 19th; it is now a hotel complete with a golf course in its grounds. Return to The Peeping Tom for refreshments.

Wildlife

A walk that passes from the Arden Parkland landscape into the typical Ancient Arden landscape. The latter is an area with distinctively small field patterns, most of which were carved out of the Forest of Arden many centuries ago to create enclosed pastures. Although hawthorn and blackthorn have been introduced to these hedges, the more ancient field boundaries also contain holly, hazel, oak, field maple, ash and even rowan.

Black Waste Wood between notes 1 and 2 is thought to be a modified remnant of the ancient Forest of Arden. Much of the oak appears to have been taken and ash now dominates and seems to have been an important coppice timber in times long past. The presence of hazel, holly, bluebell, herb robert, raspberry and other woodland species indicates that the wood is very old.

The section of dismantled railway line may not appeal to all walkers but these areas are particularly good for butterflies. The mix of habitats from shaded woodland to open grassland offers butterflies a wide variety of habitats. It attracts species such as speckled wood, orange tip and brimstone butterflies and these can be seen on warm spring days with holly blue, red admiral, peacock and tortoiseshell butterflies later into the summer.

Those taking the Route A should look out for a triangle of species rich grassland containing lesser knapweed and creeping jenny, which is now quite rare in the wild. The green lane that passes by the sub-station is particularly interesting and contains a good number of woodland plants. Walkers in the spring may be fortunate to see some of our early flowering plants such as primrose and greater stitchwort.

Greater Stitchwort

Kevin Wilkins

Burton Green Farm House

Main Walk or from station car park see p22.

1. From pub car park (see p22), **T/L** along road for 50m, cross over road to enter walkway on right. At its end x-stile, walk around field boundary in enclosed path to far right corner. X-stile on left, **fwd** hg-right to x-stile, over gap, hg-right for 120m. X-stile on right, **H/L** cross very short corner of field to x-stile, **T/R**, hg-right to x-stile at end of field. **H/R**, cross-field to x-stile in fence, **H/R** over s/b to wood boundary, **T/L**, **fwd** over sb & x-stile with wood/hg-right to go thro' k/g up to Greenway. **Fwd** over and down steps, x-stile, over s/b hg-right to go thro' gate (gap) to road.

2. **T/R** along road to junction, **T/L** along Hob Lane on pavement until it ends, continue down road until it bends right. Just after entrance to Moat Farm cross f/b & stile on left. **Fwd** cross-field over s/b (old stile), **V/R** up to x-stile in fence. **H/L** cross-field under OPL to x-double stile, hg-left to x-stile & cross-field to far left corner near lane. At stile do not cross, **T/R**, hg-left to field corner, x-stile on left, **T/R** hg-right thro' hedge gap. **T/L**, hg-left to field corner, ignore s/b and stile ahead. **T/R**, hg-left and go under OPL, thro' gap over s/b, hg-left to x-stile & s/b to road.

3. **T/R** for a short distance & **T/L** up drive to farm for 80m. **T/R** thro' f/g, hg-left, over f/b before pool, x-stile follow path barn on right, **fwd**, conifers right over f/b and pick up track to right. **T/L** along track to x-stile by large pool on right. Fc-right then hg-right to x-double stile in corner. (**Route A** see below).

4. **V/R** cross-field to Greenway. **T/L** along Greenway, for approx. 750m, passing under three bridges. 200m after third bridge **T/R** off Greenway.

5. Down steps, hg-left over small field, thro' gap (s/b) hg-left to x-stile, under OPL hg-left x-stile to track. **T/R** and shortly x-stile on right, **H/L** cross-field, thro' 2 p/g's onto narrow road next to railway. **T/R** up road, **T/L** down road and keep right at Y-junction.

6. At T-junction cross road to x-stile left of house. Thro' k/g, fence on right, **fwd** cross-field to go over stile & concrete f/b. Cross-field to x-stile, over f/b, hg-right to continue over bridge & stile, hg-right for 100m to x-stile on right. **Fwd** cross-field towards two large hedge gaps, pass thro' right hand gap to pick up hg-left & x-stiles (two) onto road. **T/R** along road using pavement to junction. **T/L** for 80m, x-double-stile on right

7. Initially cross-field and pick up hg-right, x-stile in fence ahead, hg-right to x-stile into drive. **T/R** to road, **T/L**, to cross over Lant Close, after 40m turn back up right behind houses to go over railway bridge. X-stile, **H/L** down bank cross-field to go thro' 2 k/g's & s/b, hg-left follow up and round past large conifer. Continue for 100m to x-stile on left.

8. **Fwd** cross-field to x-stile into enclosed track to road. **T/R** for The Peeping Tom or **T/L** for station.

Route A At the end of note 3, **T/L**, hg-left x-stile to go over Greenway bridge, bear round to left and follow enclosed path around sub station. X-stile, **T/R**, go over farm track, thro' k/g to pick up path between high hedges. At road **T/L** and after 80m x-stile on right. **V/R** to oak tree right of farm buildings then **V/L** to f/g at left hand field corner near farm track. Thro' f/g or x-fence stile and **fwd** up enclosed area to x-stile on left at end. **Fwd** fc-left to stile, do not cross. **T/R**, cross-field to x-stile into enclosed track to road. **T/R** for The Peeping Tom or **T/L** for station.

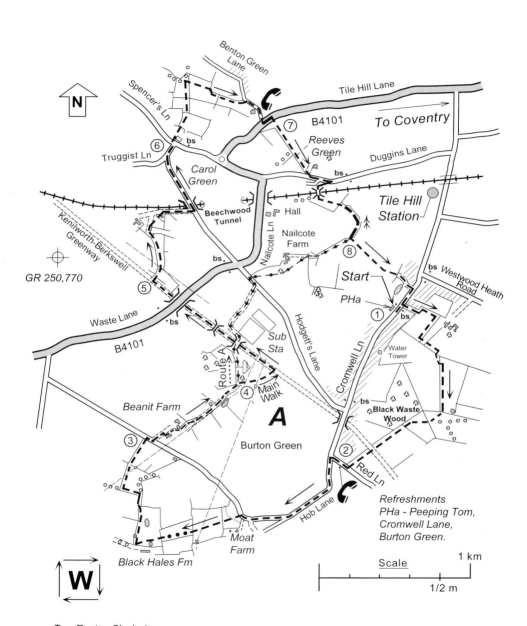

Two Routes Clockwise
Main Walk: = 7.0 m
Route A: = 4.5 m

"Around Burton Green"

Start : Kenilworth Castle car park off Castle Road.
Exiting from the Castle and car park area needs care.
Read Direction Note 1 on page 28
Grid Ref. SP 280,720
Direction : Anticlockwise
Main Walk: = 9.0 miles
Route A : = 8.0 miles
OS Maps : Landranger 140
: Pathfinder 955
: Explorer   221
Refreshments : (page 100
All in Kenilworth near start
Clarendon Arms
Queen & Castle
Tea Rooms, Castle Hill on 01926 512675
Cafe, Abbey Fields
Pub. Transport : (page 101
Kenilworth Clock nearest point to start.
12 & X17.

Parking : see above

Snippets:- *In the Autumn as you ascend through The Common this walk is spectacular. The beech tree colours are superb.*
It is well worth the visit just to see this part of Kenilworth at this time of the year.
One of the walkers who checked this route was surprised that, after passing over the bridge in Bridge Street twice every Sunday for 37 years or more and being a keen and investigative local walker, he didn't know you could walk under it.
A leaflet is available for the Kenilworth Castle Millennium Trail (1.5 miles) from WCC.

Brief Information and Outline of Route

This walk starts from the castle car park, "The Brays" in **Kenilworth** (*Chinewrde* in the DB, an enclosure of a woman called Cynehild). Cross the tilt yard bridge to what was the original entrance. The castle was probably founded by Geoffrey de Clinton in the 12th century. A mere once surrounded the castle with "The Pleasance" constructed for picnics (by Henry V) away from the castle. The castle was famously visited by Elizabeth I and written about by Sir Walter Scott. The castle was dismantled by Cromwell with only a few domestic buildings being left standing. It is now looked after by English Heritage. We now pass "Little Virginia", a community of thatched cottages, so called because potatoes are thought to have been first grown in this area.

Then onto Abbey Fields, sixty eight acres of them. The remains of St Mary's Abbey are here, built by Geoffrey de Clinton in the 12th century and demolished during the reign of Henry VIII. The church of St Nicholas close by, where Elizabeth I is said to have worshipped, is still in use. Follow Finham Brook and just before going under Townpool Bridge, look on its left side for an inscription carved above head height,

"A LARGE FLOOD 29 JULY 1834".

Follow the brook beside the new houses and over the bridge to Lower Lady's Hills to Kenilworth Common. Once quarried for sand and gravel, it became a local Nature Reserve on the 12th December 1991 (nature notes on board near entrance). At the path junction at Mill End are the old Water Works buildings, still supplying water to Kenilworth.

Up through the magnificent beech trees to join Common Lane and via the Kenilworth Road to the Kenilworth - Berkswell Greenway to Crackley. Walk north and then west to Burton Green (see page 22) pass the school in Hob Lane turn south (view of Redfern Manor) to cross Birmingham Road and up to Rudfyn Manor, its Tudor framework restored and still visible. The outbuildings are amongst the oldest in the district. The Manor was once the property of the Abbey of Kenilworth.

The walk is now at one of the highest points in Kenilworth. Cross fields to enjoy splendid views of the Castle and finally skirt the castle walls to the car park.

Wildlife

Abbey Fields holds considerable wildlife interest and includes a lake pool containing an array of wetland birds associated with this duck pond type feature. However, the pool also contains a deep wetland fringe, which attracts birds and insects to the area. Although Abbey Fields includes rough grassland the area needs time to develop a rich flora.

The other reserve is Kenilworth Common and this is probably a recently naturalised woodland. Up until the 19th century the area would have been used for grazing and therefore tree cover would have been limited. It is possible that species such as heather were present, which are now confined to the railway cutting. An area noted for its reptile population, it is the only local site known to contain all reptile species found in Warwickshire.

This walk passes through two woodland sites managed by Warwickshire Wildlife Trust. Crackley Wood is an ancient woodland which has been designated as a Local Nature Reserve and effort has been made to re-introduce ancient woodland management techniques such as coppicing. With its carpets of bluebells the subtle scent permeates the air during flowering.

Despite the seeming abundance of woodland on this walk, this is an area where recent woodland loss has been extensive. This includes the north of Crackley Wood, the felling and partial replanting of Rough Knowles Wood and the eradication of Long Meadows Wood, which used to extend almost up to Hob Lane.

The string of ponds that run from Rudfyn Manor to Kenilworth Castle all appear to be drying out. It is possible that this is partly due to the over abstraction of water from the area.

Around Kenilworth Castle grassland are species such as lesser knapweed, harebell, lady's bedstraw and bird's foot trefoil. Tall yellow spikes of great mullein can be found on the disturbed banks of the Finham Brook in this area.

Kenilworth Castle

Kevin Wilkins

Main Walk (Take care exiting from Castle and car park area)

1. Walk along the causeway towards the castle, **T/R** down steps just before metal gates. Follow round with castle walls on left to the k/g that leads to main road. **For safety T/L for 50m or so away from corner, before crossing busy road. T/R** along pavement, passing Queen & Castle and Castle and Tea Rooms. Cross over Elizabeth Way. Shortly past Malthouse Lane **T/R** to cross over road & go down surfaced footpath into Abbey Fields. Leave surfaced path when wall corner comes in on right, **T/R**, wall left, down, thro' edge of small copse to the bottom with buildings on your left, lake on your right. **Fwd** over bridge, immediately **T/L, fwd** stream left to to **T/L** over metal bridge. **T/R**, leave path, **fwd** fence left & stream right to pass under road (if flooded go over road). Shortly over another f/b to follow path to junction with School Lane.

2. **T/L** & then shortly **T/L** again (over road bridge) after 100m **T/R** up narrow passage between gardens (care on exit), **T/R** along road to enter The Common. After 70m, at information board, **T/L** to take uphill bridle path that soon curves right, keep **fwd** on bridle path where footpath crosses & continue to Common Lane.

3. **T/L** & then at Coventry Road **T/R**, down road & at end of houses on your left, **T/L** into cart track, thro' k/g on right, up slope to the Berkswell-Kenilworth Greenway. (**Route A** see below). Continue **fwd** to go under left span of first bridge & up steps to x-stile. **T/L** over bridge & follow bridle path **fwd** with boundary on left, thro' two gates, **fwd** to f/b over stream & up enclosed path to road.

4. Over road, down enclosed bridle path opposite to go thro' p/g into enclosed area. **Fwd** over culvert to x-stile, just past bridle gate on right. **V/L** cross-field to go thro' p/g & **V/L** cross-field to junction with farm track at f/g. **Do not go over stile.** With back to stile, **fwd** up farm track to first hedge coming in on right. Thro' k/g on right, **H/L** cross-field to hedge line, keep hedge on right, & follow thro' p/g & s/b to road.

5. **T/R** along road until it turns sharp right. Thro' k/g on left, right of gate, **T/R**, hg-right to x-stile, cross-field aiming for wood and passing the farm buildings on your left by 30m to x-stile near end of field, x-stile continue **fwd** to meet boundary with wood coming in on your right. X-stile, hg-right to go **fwd** over Greenway via k/g & stile, continue **fwd**, hg-right to road.

6. **T/R** along road & then **T/L** into Hob Lane. Along pavement, (passing school) until it ends approx. 500m. **T/L** & enter drive, immediately **T/R** down narrow walkway. Keeping boundary on left follow through copse to x-stile. **Fwd** to meet hedge coming in on right. Continue to corner & x-stile, **V/L** until you see the opposite hedge line. Aim for stile left of centre & go over stream & x-stile. **H/L** cross-field corner to go through gap, **T/R**, with hg-right thro' k/g onto main road.

7. Over **busy** road, **fwd** up drive towards Rudfyn Manor. Top of drive, just before Manor, **T/L** (WMP) **fwd** to go thro' hedge gap. **T/R**, hg-right, follow round left to outward hedge corner. **Fwd** cross-field to hedge ahead, **T/L**, hg-right, under OPL, at field corner **T/R**, hg-left, pass pool on left to hedge gap. **T/L** thro' gap, hg-left, at bend in hedge **T/R**, cross-field to gap in hedge. **Fwd** cross-field to top RH corner of small copse. Thro' copse, hg-right to another small copse, pool left, cross s/b **T/R**, hg-right thro' k/g into Chase Lane.

8. **T/R** & shortly thro' k/g on left, **H/L**, cross-field thro' k/g in field corner. **T/L**, hg-left to field corner. Thro' k/g, thro' small copse, pool right, **H/R** cross-field towards castle. Thro' k/g, keep on same line to gate gap on right of ruin. **H/L** thro' k/g leading to lane, **T/L** & then after 130m x-stile on right just before thatched cottage. Keep castle wall on left to go thro' k/g, **T/R** along lower path to car park.

Route A The route can be shortened by using the Greenway. After joining it during direction 3 continue on it for nearly 3km (look out for Black Waste Wood on right) to **T/L**, hg-right to road. Continue with Note 6.

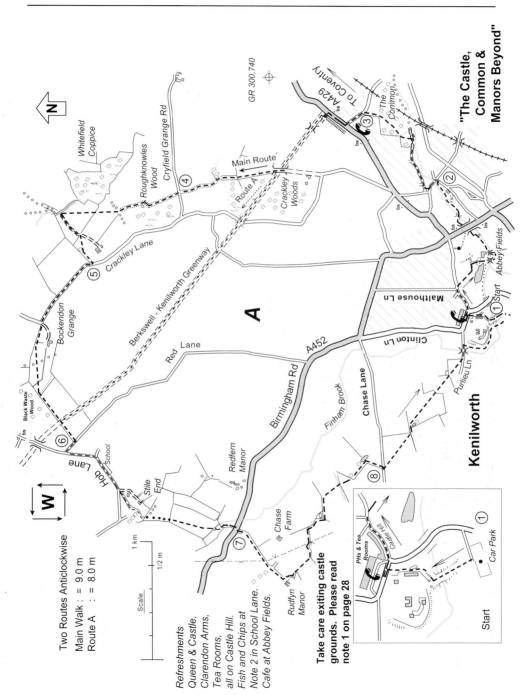

N

W

Whitefield Coppice

Roughknowles Wood

Cryfield Grange Rd

GR 300,740

A429 To Coventry

The Common

④

Main Route

Route A

Crackley Woods

③

②

Crackley Lane

Berkswell - Kenilworth Greenway

⑤

Bockendon Grange

Red Lane

A

A452

Birmingham Rd

Finham Brook

Malthouse Ln

Clinton Ln

Abbey Fields

Purliey Ln

Kenilworth

Black Waste Wood

Hob Lane

School

⑥

Stile End

Redfern Manor

Chase Lane

⑧

Chase Farm

⑦

Rudfyn Manor

"The Castle, Common & Manors Beyond"

① Start

Two Routes Anticlockwise

Main Walk : = 9.0 m
Route A   : = 8.0 m

Scale
1 km
1/2 m

Refreshments
Queen & Castle,
Clarendon Arms,
Tea Rooms,
all on Castle Hill.
Fish and Chips at
Note 2 in School Lane.
Cafe at Abbey Fields.

Take care exiting castle grounds. Please read note 1 on page 28

PHs & Tea Rooms

Castle Hill

① Car Park

Start

Start : War Memorial Park
        Coventry
Grid Ref. SP 321,773
Direction : Anticlockwise
Main Walk: = 12.0 miles
Route A : = 7.0 miles
OS Maps : Landranger 140
        : Pathfinder 955
        : Explorer 221
Refreshments : (page 100
Burnt Post, Kenpas Highway
The Festival, Stivichall.
The Oak, The Mill, Baginton
Stoneleigh Village Club
Pub. Transport : (page 101
Start Park & Ride South,
X12, X16 & X18.
On or near route X17,
538 & 539.
Parking : Public Car Park.

Snippets:-

The former school at Baginton was founded by Lucy Price in 1814 to support the "poorest inhabitants of the village". Some of the private gardens of Stoneleigh and Baginton are occasionally opened to the public under the National Gardens Scheme.

The meadow where the Sherbourne joins the Sowe is readily accessed by following the path and riverside just over the bridge from The Mill at Baginton.

From collected poems and epigrams of George Hamilton.

"To Town? His plodding mare and rumbling tyres

Roll on to Coventry, city of spires,

Ribbons and bicycles, where Peeping Tom

Hopes the white shade Godiva still may come."

On route A the walk down Kenilworth Road is described as the finest approach to any city in the British Isles.

Brief Information and Outline of Route

Starting in **Coventry** (*Couentre* in 1043 and *Couentreu* in the DB, tree of a man called Cofa), at the War Memorial Park officially opened in 1921 and the City's War Memorial unveiled by Field Marshal Earl Haig in 1927. Then through the trees lining the Kenilworth Road to Canley Ford, worn deep by the passage of vehicles over hundreds of years and once the main route from Allesley to Stivichall village. There are signs of quarrying on the right hand side.

Now through Canley Ford, Coventry's only Millennium Green, comprising three hay meadows maintained in a traditional manner (page 103). In the first meadow on the left can be seen the Kestrel by Walenty Pytel. At the western boundary of the small meadow and copse adjacent to the A45 there are twenty plus concrete cylindrical blocks used as obstacles on the A45 to prevent enemy aircraft from using the road as a landing strip during the 1940 invasion scare. Follow Canley Brook then through Tocil Wood, university sports fields and farmland to the outskirts of Kenilworth.

Cross the golf course, riding school, A46 and round to **Stoneleigh** village. (*Stanlei* in the DB, stony woodland clearing). Down the hill to the River Sowe (*Sowa* in the DB pre English river name) past the Norman Church of St Mary the Virgin across Stoneleigh Meadows created by the villagers into a Trust for the public in 1982.

Then along the main road towards Coventry past the old site of a petrol station and Co-op that was formally one of two mills in the village. Cross the river and pass Coventry's sewage works on the left bank. Follow the River Sowe to **Baginton** (*Badechitone* in the DB, estate of a man named Badeca) up the hill to the 13th century church of St John the Baptist, time for a rest to admire the fine view. The rectory and school (now closed) are nearby. Beyond the church but in private fields are the ruins of a 14th century castle destroyed by fire in 1706. Through the churchyard, with wonderful views and memories of comrades lost in the last war and across the "park", these were the elegant grounds of Baginton Hall, destroyed by fire in 1889. Continue to Mill Hill, to the right uphill is the renowned reconstruction of the Lunt Roman Fort.

Turn down Mill Hill to The Old Mill Hotel, once a working mill, and opposite is Russell's Garden Centre. If you wish to visit the confluence of the Sherbourne (*Scireburne* in DB, a bright or clear stream) and Sowe, turn right after bridge along footpath and keep river on right as near as is practical. Make your way back to the main walk by aiming for the roundabout at the junction of A45/A46 and through a gap in the hedge adjacent to footpaths leading to underpass and footbridges over this busy junction.

On approaching the War Memorial Park you go through Stivichall Hamlet, passing the Gregory Hood memorial and the old Smithy probably built in the 18th century. Under the railway bridge built in 1842 with the Gregory (then the landowner) coat of arms on both sides. Near the bridge on the left side of the road is an old animal pound first recorded in 1663. The Stivichall Hamlet was acquired for preservation by Coventry Council in 1929 and includes the Smithy and several cottages.

Coat of Arms Bridge

Wildlife

An early morning stroll suitable for all times of the year but perhaps most enjoyable in the early part of the summer. On leaving the War Memorial Park you enter an old woodland with numerous old oak trees and often containing young ash, elm and frequent mature holly and hawthorn. Open access to the woods has damaged the woodland flora which contains bramble, bracken, rosebay willowherb, ivy and woodland grasses. More oak woodland is to be found after crossing over Kenilworth Road, this area is less disturbed and includes hazel, rowan, aspen, wood avens, ferns and hedge woundwort.

The path then passes through Canley Ford which is flanked by a series of rich grasslands. Species include bird's foot trefoil, great burnet, lesser knapweed, pignut, meadow vetchling, cat's ear, ox-eye daisy, lady's bedstraw and musk mallow.

On crossing the A45 and following the course of Canley Brook the early risers may be rewarded by the punctuated "plop!" of a water vole as it drops from the brook's bank into the water to escape a potential predator. Once a very common species on British waters the water vole is now nearing extinction in Britain due to the introduction of mink. We are fortunate therefore to have a very healthy population on our doorstep.

As you follow the Canley Brook down towards the University of Warwick (Coventry), summer wanderers will be drawn by the opulent pink and aroma of the himalayan balsam. This impressive plant is an introduced species which has spread along many British waterways and is thought by many to be an invasive pest. On through the new Gibbet Hill Wood, which was planted in 1999 by local people, students and girl guides, in partnership with The Woodland Trust, University of Warwick and Coventry's Countryside Project.

Eventually, you enter into Tocil Wood the remnant of an ancient oak woodland containing frequent sycamore with hawthorn, hazel, holly and rowan. The wood includes areas that used to flood and contain alder, ferns, sedges, bugle and a localised invasion of himalayan balsam.

On the outskirts of Kenilworth the path passes along the side of Kenilworth Common, a Warwickshire Wildlife Trust reserve noted for its reptile populations. This partially wooded area used to contain adders but none have been recorded for many years. Going north of Stoneleigh the path follows the River Sowe. It is sometimes possible to see signs where badgers have been foraging within the rough pastures along the banks of the river. Badgers are particularly fond of worms and use their powerful front claws to open the turf in search of such delicacies. If walking during the summer keep an eye open for banded demoiselle, a large colourful damselfly. This species is particularly associated with emergent common club-rush (or bulrush) because the aquatic larval stage uses this plant to escape the water prior to emergence.

Main Walk

1. Leave Park & Ride by the p/g into the copse adjacent to the Kenilworth Rd. **T/L** thro' copse, keep parallel to main road, look for pedestrian crossing lights on right and cross to other side. **T/L** and then shortly **T/R** into Canley Ford. **Fwd** passing allotments on left. Where lane turns right keep **fwd** thro' wooden bollards down green lane to pass the ford on your left. Continue up the lane to the A45 and garage. Cross A45 using pedestrian crossing.

2. **T/L** for 250m to cross over Canley Brook (248 70Q), shortly **T/R** down bank, keep brook on your right **fwd** to Cannon Hill Rd. **Fwd** over road with brook right, when a f/b is reached, don't cross over, **T/L** hg-right, in 20m **T/R** thro' gap & over f/b, **fwd** thro' young copse to hedge gap ahead. Hg-right after 70m **T/R** into Tocil Wood thro' second gap, keep left on path until you reach Cycleway. **T/R** down to just past the Lakes, **T/L** with lake on left **fwd** to x-stile onto road. Opposite and just to the left, x-stile, keep stream on left, **fwd** thro' gap to pool, keep round pool on your right, **T/L** over f/b. **T/R**, with hg-left, brook right **fwd** to go over another f/b on right, **T/L** to shortly reach the main footbridge set back on your left.

3. Up & over f/b, bear left and **fwd** hg-left to reach road. Thro' k/g opposite, **fwd** with hg-right to go thro' gap in fence. **Fwd** on track, with hg-left & lone tree on right over culvert. **Fwd** on the track with hg-fc-left until field corner thro' gap (WMP), **H/L,** hg-right uphill. At field corner **T/R** thro' gap, **T/L** x-stile, fwd hg-left over two fields. To exit thro' k/g and climb up onto Greenway. **T/L** & in 100m down slope on right, thro' k/g to road. (**Route A** see below).

4. At road **T/R** & then second **L** down Common Ln. Over bridge & pass shops to the junction, **T/R** & then **T/L** to go up Knowle Hill. Immediately above Frythe Cl. **T/L** to follow Waymark signs thro' fenced walkway & golf course. Cross last fairway to stile hidden on return hedge opposite. X-stile, **T/L** & cross-field just right of farmhouse to track. Cross-field to exit onto another track via stile. **Fwd** to follow Waymark signs thro' Riding School to boundary of Warwick Bypass. X-stile on left, **fwd** with bypass right, x-stile & another field to x-stile to steps on right leading up to road. This is a **busy** junction of roads & bypass connections.

5. Over bypass & continue down road (pavement left). At junction **T/R** & in 40m thro' k/g on left, **T/R** hg-right **fwd** thro' k/g, **fwd** hg-right to k/g (do not go thro'). **T/L** cross-field to go thro' k/g off field corner, hg-left, thro' k/g into walkway to road.

6. **Fwd** across road down tarmac track to bridge over river. Do not cross river, **T/L** thro' gate, follow river bank and when level with church **H/L** to main road near bridge. **T/L** & follow main road round to right for 350m (cross road carefully). Just past detached house **T/R** thro' k/g & f/g to cross the Sowe via two footbridges. **T/L**, keeping river left, thro' k/g & then hg-right thro' k/g in this hedge. **T/L** river left now passing thro' a series of seven fields via k/g's keeping field boundaries and sewage works extension on left. **T/L** in front of metal gate. Over slab bridge up past cottages on right towards the church at Baginton. **T/L** & then **T/R** thro' churchyard, **T/R** & **T/L**, fwd fc-left down track, **V/L** down entry fronting detached houses to the main road. **T/R** & **T/L** down main road to go over the bridge (River Sowe).

7. Pass under by-pass bridge & immediately **T/R** up pathway, at top **T/L** go round right over pedestrian bridge. Follow under A45 subway on left & **fwd** to cross pedestrian bridge leading to Leaf Lane. **T/R** & then immediately **T/L** into Fenside Ave.

8. **Fwd** to Baginton Rd. **T/R** & walk up to junction with Leamington Rd. Cross road using pedestrian crossing (on left) **T/R, T/L** to continue down final part of Baginton Rd. Just before joining Stivichall Croft enter copse on left, **V/R** to monument. Under Coat of Arms Bridge & continue on pavement to School entrance. Cross road to enter park & **fwd** to start area.

Route A At end of Note 3 **T/L** along pavement for approx. 1.7km, **fwd** over Gibbet Hill Rd. towards the city for approx. 1.4km, to Cannon Hill Rd, cross to other side & after approx. 300m on right go thro' a spinney path to Woodside Ave. **T/L** up to A45 & **T/R** up to cross A45 at pedestrian crossing near shops. Down Wainbody Ave (N) to Green Ln. **T/L** to Coat of Arms Bridge Rd. **T/R** and enter park on left, **H/L** across park to start area.

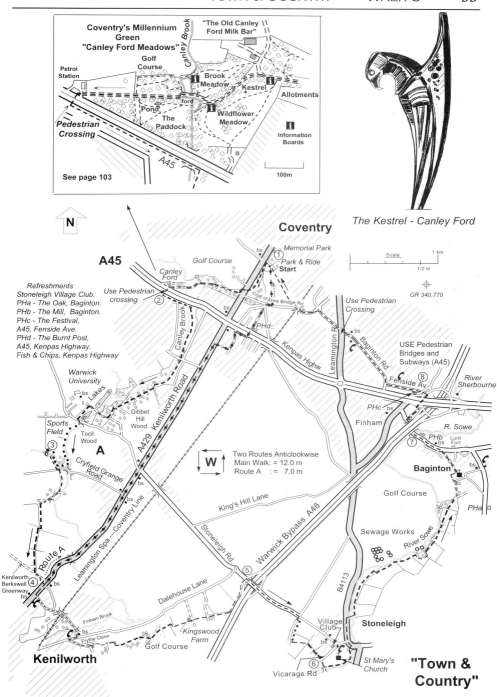

Inset map — Coventry's Millennium Green

Coventry's Millennium Green
"Canley Ford Meadows"

Canley Brook

"The Old Canley Ford Milk Bar"

Golf Course

Petrol Station

Brook Meadow

Kestrel

Allotments

Pedestrian Crossing

Pond

ford

The Paddock

Wildflower Meadow

Information Boards

A45

See page 103

100m

The Kestrel - Canley Ford

N

Coventry

A45

Golf Course

Canley Ford

Memorial Park
Park & Ride
Start ①

Use Pedestrian crossing ②

Refreshments
Stoneleigh Village Club.
PHa - The Oak, Baginton.
PHb - The Mill, Baginton.
PHc - The Festival,
A45, Fenside Ave.
PHd - The Burnt Post,
A45, Kenpas Highway.
Fish & Chips, Kenpas Highway.

Coat of Arms Bridge Rd
PHd

Canley Brook

Kenpas Highw

Leamington R

Use Pedestrian Crossing

Baginton Rd

USE Pedestrian Bridges and Subways (A45)

Fenside Av ⑧

River Sherbourne

Warwick University

Lakes

Gibbet Hill Wood

Kenilworth Road

A429

PHc

Finham

PHb

Lunt Fort

R. Sowe

Sports Field

Tocil Wood

③

A

Cryfield Grange Road

⑦

Baginton

Golf Course

PHa

W

Two Routes Anticlockwise
Main Walk: = 12.0 m
Route A : = 7.0 m

King's Hill Lane

Sewage Works

River Sowe

Leamington Spa - Coventry Line

Stoneleigh Rd

Warwick Bypass A46

B4113

Route A

Kenilworth Berkswell Greenway ④

⑤

Dalehouse Lane

Village Club

Stoneleigh

Finham Brook

Kingswood Farm

Frythe Close

Golf Course

⑥

Vicarage Rd

St Mary's Church

Kenilworth

Scale
1 km
1/2 m

GR 340,770

"Town & Country"

© Crown Copyright

Start : Vicarage Road
Stoneleigh
Grid Ref. SP 328,726
Direction: see map
Main Walk: = 3.5 miles
OS Maps : Landranger 140
**   : Pathfinder 955**
**   : Explorer 221**
Refreshments : (page 100
Village Club, Stoneleigh
Pub. Transport : (page 101
To Stoneleigh, Stareton
538 & 539 (Mon to Sat)
Parking : Carefully in village
ensuring that you do not
block any driveway or
access.

Brief Information and Outline of Route

Starting at Vicarage Road, **Stoneleigh** (*Stanlei* in DB, a stony woodland clearing) on the River Sowe (*Sowa* in the DB pre English river name). It has a Norman Church and a well known Smithy on the village green with a distinctive horseshoe built into its brick structure. The village had a pub in the 19th century but it was closed by Lord Leigh after his daughter had been whistled at by "lads who had cycled out from Coventry!" There is now a club, the old village gaol, where you can buy refreshments. Opposite are the alms-houses built by Lady Leigh in the 17th century.

Cross the Sowe by a footbridge passing the restored cottages up to Motslow Hill named from *moot* or meeting place. Its quarry provided stone for the church and alms houses. There is a good viewing point, on private land that overlooks the village and Coventry beyond on the top of Motlsow Hill. Cross Leamington Road and the parkland with its old oak trees, down over a packhorse bridge and then a footbridge over the River Avon (from a Celtic word meaning river).

Then uphill to the hamlet of **Stareton**. Thomas Sotherne of *Starton*, left in his will of 1625 twenty shillings yearly to the poor of *Starton* and to the repair of *Starton* footbridge leading to the church at *Stoneley*. Turn right to Stoneleigh Abbey estate founded in the 12th century, now the NAC (National Agricultural Centre), north to cross the Avon again using the 14th century Stare Bridge.

Duncan Bean

Stare Bridge

Down the steep hill to the junction left over the 19th century bridge and through the Norman St. Mary-the-Virgin's churchyard. Across the field then up the track to Vicarage Lane. Pass Wentworth House, once Stoneleigh Vicarage, cross the fields slightly uphill where views of Sowe Mouth (confluence of Rivers Sowe and Avon) can be seen. North along the road and back down across fields to join an enclosed path back to the village.

Wildlife

With a name like Stoneleigh you would perhaps be expecting some association with rock and this seems to be the case as almost everywhere you look there are small quarries. Most of these are now water filled and it's often difficult to separate the farm ponds from the quarries. The area also contains a network of watercourses and includes the confluence between the River Sowe and the River Avon. These rivers would also have offered up considerable opportunities for quarrying.

Water quality in the River Sowe is much improved with improvements to the Finham Sewage Works to the north. When crossing rivers you may be fortunate enough to hear the characteristic peep and the small flash of blue, which indicates that you've just seen a kingfisher (or indeed a kingfisher has just seen you!)

Narrow bands of oak woodland are complemented by much larger woodland blocks on level ground. Invariably these areas of predominantly oak woodland include a range of tree species not native to the area such as sycamore, horse chestnut, pine, beech and grey poplar. Elm, holly and willow are also well represented in the area and the woods often contain a wide variety of woodland herbs such as enchanter's nightshade, herb robert, woody nightshade and red campion.

Although all pasture, the grassland tends to be agriculturally improved with only small areas of grassland that might support an array of wild species. Some areas where tree felling appears to have taken place are generally quite rich and contain wetland species such as meadowsweet rushes and tall grasses.

Maureen Harris

Sowe Mouth

This is a sketch from a winter photograph. The Rivers Sowe (foreground) and Avon are running full. (The walkers taking a rest, are shown off the ROW.)

1. Go down surfaced path opposite Holly House and cross f/b over the River Sowe. Follow up through enclosed path that turns right and left to go thro' k/g. **Fwd**, fc-left and continue on same line for 150m to pass right hand side of fenced pool, turn **H/L** to go thro' k/g's and small copse to road.

2. **T/R** along road for 100m to go thro' k/g on other side of road. **H/R** to shortly go thro' k/g, **H/R** on same line cross-field and go down over small stone bridge and then a f/b over the River Avon. Cross surfaced track and **fwd** up hill, hg/fc-left thro' copse to gain road thro' two gates (Stareton).

3. **T/R** along road for approx. 500m to junction.

4. At junction cross over road to NAC entrance. Immediately **T/R** into the old road and go thro' k/g & over Stare Bridge, continue up to go thro' k/g to main road. **T/L** along verge for 200m and go thro' k/g on left, **fwd** thro' copse to go thro' k/g ahead. **T/R**, copse boundary on right for 350m (crossing over NAC vehicle access), **T/R** thro' k/g's (used earlier) onto main road. **T/L** and walk along pavement & down to the bottom of the hill.

5. **T/L** over road bridge (pedestrian bridge on opposite side). Cross back over road to go thro' gate at end of bridge. At this point you can <u>either</u> follow the river bank (Stoneleigh Meadow) or the Right of Way that goes thro' the church yard. For the river bank **H/L**, thro' fence gap and follow riverbank to go thro' p/g to fenced track. [For the church continue **fwd** fc-right to go thro' p/g to road. **Fwd** along road, go thro' churchyard to exit at p/g. Follow maintained path thro' p/g to fenced track]. **T/R** up to Vicarage Rd. and then **T/L** to go thro' k/g ahead on the left of gate to Wentworth House. Keep house boundary on your right for approx. 50m, **fwd** on same line to fence ahead to go thro' k/g. **H/R** up cross-field to go thro' p/g, **fwd** thro' a belt of trees to roadside.

6. **T/R** along verge for 250m, just past vehicle entrance to NAC, go thro' k/g.

7. **Fwd** cross-field to go thro' k/g, <u>off</u> field corner. Hg-left to go thro' k/g into enclosed footpath. Follow down to Vicarage Road.

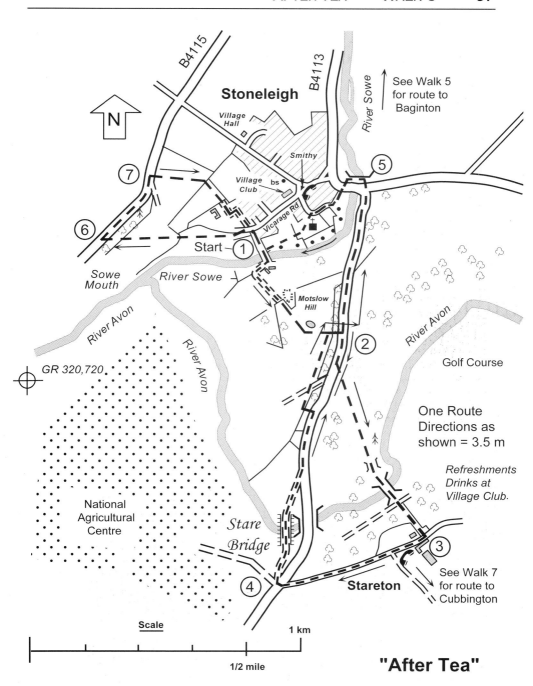

N

B4115

B4113

River Sowe

Stoneleigh

Village Hall

Smithy

See Walk 5 for route to Baginton

⑤

Village Club   bs

Vicarage Rd

⑦

⑥

Start   ①

Sowe Mouth

River Sowe

River Avon

River Avon

Motslow Hill

②

River Avon

Golf Course

GR 320,720

One Route Directions as shown = 3.5 m

Refreshments Drinks at Village Club.

National Agricultural Centre

Stare Bridge

③

④   **Stareton**

See Walk 7 for route to Cubbington

Scale

1 km

1/2 mile

"After Tea"

© Crown Copyright

Start : Old school in lay-by at Bubbenhall
Grid Ref. SP 363,722
Direction : Clockwise
Main Walk: = 9.0 miles
Route A : = 3.5 miles
OS Maps : (p = part)
: Landranger 140p
: Landranger 151p
: Pathfinder 955p
: Pathfinder 976p
: Explorer 221
Refreshments : ✆ page 100
Malt Shovel & Three Horse-shoes, Bubbenhall
King's Head, Cubbington
The Bull, Weston under Wetherley
Pub. Transport : ✆ page 101
Start 538 & 539 bus from Coventry to Bubbenhall or train to Leamington then bus to Cubbington 68.
Parking : In lay-by

Snippets:-
There is a brewery in Cubbington, The Warwickshire Beer Company. It started up in 1998 in the former bakery near the centre of the village.
The saw mills, an ever present and visible business for over a 100 years has relocated to near Leamington Spa.
The main sewage was not connected to the village until after the Second World War. Apparently men of the village were known as "Cubbington Earbiters" following a soccer match incident, some years ago, when a lad had his ear lobe bitten off.
Mr Horace Lloyd was awarded the BEM for the work his team of firemen did during the Coventry Blitz 14th November 1940.

Brief Information and Outline of Route

Starting at the old school in **Bubbenhall** go down a driveway to negotiate the quarry's conveyor belts southwards. The path diverted now in places round the sand and gravel/landfill quarry. Here you walk in the footsteps of prehistoric man. Waverley Wood Farm Pit has been recognised as a Palaeolithic site of considerable importance and finds of stone tools, mammal bones, plant fossils etc., have been recorded, some of which may be seen in Warwick Museum.

Manor Cottage - Cubbington

At **Weston under Wetherley** pass St Michael's Church and across the fields to **Cubbington** (*Cobintone* in DB, estate of a man called Cubba). The village lies in a shallow valley on a stream, a tributary of the Leam. It has a Norman church of St Mary, where Jane Austen's brother was vicar.

During the Second World War many evacuees came from Coventry, Birmingham and London to stay in the village.

The Old Manor House - Cubbington

Now walk towards the hamlet of **Stareton** (see page 34), and then on past Tantara Lodge, the old entrance to what was Stoneleigh Deer Park.

Kevin Wilkins

Restored Barn

Across fields passing a restored barn back to **Bubbenhall**, on high ground beside the Avon known in DB as *"Bubenhalle"* and in Saxon times as *"Bubenhull"*, hill of a man called Bubba. Also, according to stories told to the children in the old village school *"Bubbling hole"* due to the large number of natural springs to be found in the village.

Pass through St Giles' churchyard. The church was initially built in the 12th century of local Keupers stone, with a number of additions made in the 14th century. It had a new peal of six bells installed in time for the Millennium celebrations. The 12th century font was believed to have been used as an animal water trough at one time! Sadly, the church has to be kept locked, though a key can be obtained from a nearby resident.

Pass Church House, thought possibly to have been the Prebendal Mansion to the parish church of St Giles. The prominent Manor House, at the junction with Stoneleigh Road, is a relatively recent property built on the site of a much older building.

Off route to the left one passes through a pleasing mix of new and old buildings, from the 17th century timbered Malt Shovel public house, Yew Tree Farm, the Old Forge and Victoria Cottages.

Continue on the route past Bubbenhall's second public house, The Three Horseshoes. In the wall opposite, under an ancient oak tree, can be seen "The Spout". Until the middle of the last century this was an important water supply for the whole village, never known to have dried up. Claimed by many people, both local and not so local, to be excellent drinking water. It was only in the decade 1980 to 1990 that it was declared unsuitable for drinking due to its high nitrate levels. However, there are still those who swear that their cuppa wouldn't be the same if made with any other water! Sadly, due to sand and gravel extraction, the flow is diminishing.

Wildlife

This walk is dominated by an extensive area of woodland running north to south and includes Waverley Wood, Weston Wood, North Cubbington Wood and South Cubbington Wood and represents an almost continuous expanse of woodland over three kilometres in length. Unfortunately, most of the woodland here is plantation, with only the southern section of Weston Wood and South Cubbington Wood being semi-natural.

Weston Wood is arguably the most renowned woodland in the area in that it is here that for many years it was assumed that the only Warwickshire population of dormice occurred. In more recent times surveys have suggested that this species occurs in a number of Warwickshire woodlands and efforts are underway to try and establish the true distribution of this shy and rarely seen creature.

Walkers will immediately see that the area is also heavily affected by gravel extraction operations. Such work has in the past created areas such as Brandon Marsh and it is hoped that restoration of the site will offer opportunities for the establishment of interesting wildlife habitats. Whilst works continue Bubbenhall Wood has been chosen as an experimental site for the re-establishment of dormice to the wood.

South Cubbington Wood appears to be dominated by oak in the north and ash in the south. It is extremely rich with a number of rare plants including ancient stands of wild service tree, midland hawthorn and small leaved lime. Townhall clock can also be seen from the footpath as well as bluebell and wood anemone.

Main Walk

1. With back to old school go left for 100m, thro' p/g (in f/g) on left. **Fwd** along road thro' fenced quarry workings until near boundary of wood, x-bridge over conveyor. **T/R**, keep wood on left, x-stile on left and follow round in enclosed path to the end. **T/R**, hg-right to field corner, x-stile on left. **Fwd** along enclosed path to end, x-stile on right into field. With fence on right continue to electricity pole near end of field. **H/R**, still with fc-right to enter enclosed path and copse / hg-left. Follow round until path ends. **T/L** x-stile, s/b, x-stile **T/R** stream right, shortly x-stile & f/b. **Fwd** hg-right to x-stile onto road. **T/R** for 250m. (**Route A** see below).

2. **T/L**, over s/b, x-stile, **V/L** "plus" cross-field to outward hedge corner. **H/L**, thro' gap in hedge ahead. **T/R**, hg-right to field corner, over s/b into next field. **H/L**, look up field to far hedge line & aim uphill cross-field for small gap just right of prominent tree. Go thro' gap & **fwd** cross-field to go thro' left side of large hedge gap. A short distance away go thro' smaller gap on left (WMP), **T/R** to pick up hg-right. **Fwd** over 3 fields hg-right to x-stile onto road.

3. **T/L** down road (pavement) for 150m. **T/R** opposite church thro' gap, wall/fc/hg-left to x-stile in corner. Cross narrow field to go over f/b. **T/R**, stream then hg/fc-right to farm track. **T/L**, up track for 40m **T/R** fc/hg-right for 70m to **T/R** over f/b. **Fwd** hg-left ignore f/b just before wood. Just after, enter wood thro' gap on left & follow path up thro' wood with ditch on left to exit just past s/b. **T/L** wood left, follow round right, hg-left down to field corner & over f/b. **T/L** follow hg/fc-left round to right to "path T junction". (Note **T/L** here for The King's Head and village). **T/R**, **fwd** cross-field and gap to road.

4. Cross road (WMP) thro' gap, **fwd** to meet hedge line ahead and go thro' gap to pick up hg-left for two fields then **T/R**, hg-left to meet corner of wood. **T/L** and keep wood on right until WMP, fc-right to go over f/b in hedgeline. **T/L**, hg-left (enclosed path) to x-stile and s/b to road.

5. Opposite, x-stile into enclosed path, <u>keep</u> **fwd** x-stiles (3), & over two farm tracks to road. **T/L** and shortly **T/R** up farm track to the road at Stareton.

6. **T/R** along road (ACW) for approx. 1 km, **T/L** at road junction and then after 400m **T/R** at Tantara Lodge, 200m from junction, at spinney **T/R** over f/b into enclosed path. With hg-right to field corner x-double stile. **Fwd** hg-right to x-stile.
   Fwd hg-right for approx. 100m to **T/L** at WMP.

7. Aim for "out of sight" top right hand field corner, x-stile in corner. **Fwd** with fence and gate on left for 15m, **T/L**, x-stile, hg-left to x-stile off field corner. With pool on left, **H/R** cross-field, aiming to left of house, cross a farm track (with stiles), then x-stile in corner next to garden into road. Cross road and go thro' k/g, **H/R** to x-stile in hedge a short distance away, **T/L** up hg-left for 70m and x-stile on left. **T/R**, hg-right up thro' field to x-stile into a fenced walkway around a large garden on left and then a disused quarry on right Follow down drive to road. **T/L** down road for 250m and **T/R** thro' k/g. **T/R** up enclosed path, hg-right to x-stile, **T/L** and descend with conifer hedge on left to x-stile into field, cross-field, thro' p/g aiming for church, enter churchyard and exit at front gate. **Fwd** up road to junction, continue **fwd** passing "Three Horseshoes" on left, go right at Y-junction (Pit Hill) up to main road. **T/L** to old school house.

Route A

At the end of Note 1 continue up road for another 200m. At "Road Narrows" sign **T/L** & follow path along edge of wood to reach enclosed path & gravel drive to road. Over road & x-stile opposite, hg-left to field corner, x-stile hg-left to next field corner. X-double-stile, **fwd** and in a short distance **T/R** at WMP, continue with Note 7.

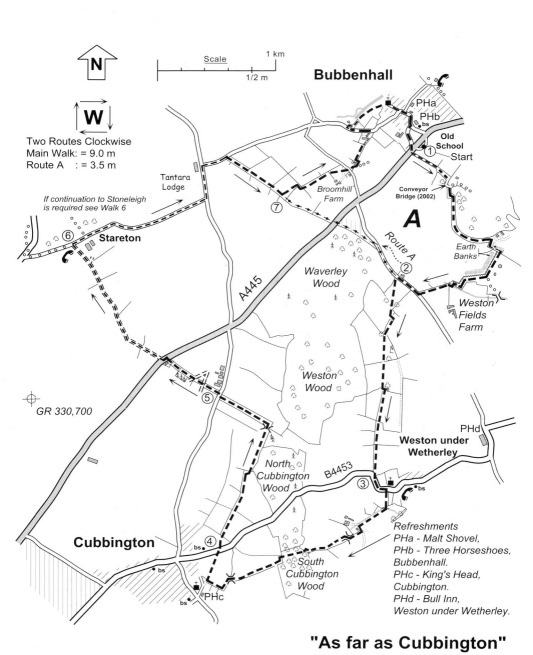

Two Routes Clockwise
Main Walk: = 9.0 m
Route A   : = 3.5 m

If continuation to Stoneleigh is required see Walk 6

GR 330,700

Refreshments
PHa - Malt Shovel,
PHb - Three Horseshoes,
Bubbenhall.
PHc - King's Head,
Cubbington.
PHd - Bull Inn,
Weston under Wetherley.

"As far as Cubbington"

Start : Lay-by adjacent to old school on A445
Grid Ref. SP 363,722
Direction : Anticlockwise
Main Walk: = 10.0 miles
Route A : = 8.5 miles
OS Maps : (p = part)
: Landranger 140p
: Landranger 151p
: Pathfinder 955p
: Pathfinder 956p
: Explorer 221p
: Explorer 222p
Refreshments : (page 100
Oak & Black Dog,
Stretton on Dunsmore
Shoulder of Mutton,
Stretton on Dunsmore
Blacksmith's Arms,
Ryton on Dunsmore
Malt Shovel,
Bubbenhall
Three Horseshoes,
Bubbenhall
Three Horseshoes,
Princethorpe
Pub. Transport : (a page 101
To Bubbenhall 538 & 539
On or near route 570 & 580
Parking : Large Lay-by.

Snippets:-
Apparently Sir William Lyons would confirm the lines of any new or modified Jaguar body shape by having them parked on his drive at Wappenbury Hall.
The elegant setting enabled him to make a sound judgement before giving the nod for it to go into production.
Ryton Pools Country Park with its pools and woodland trails can be easily accessed by walking towards Coventry on the large verge for 300m from the junction of Paget's Lane and the A445 to a pedestrian gate.

Brief Information and Outline of Route

Starting at the old school, now closed, in **Bubbenhall** (see page 38) walk down the drive past the now derelict Glebe Farm to meet the conveyor belts near the sand and gravel quarries. Turn south to Wappenbury (*Wapeberie* in the DB, stronghold of a man called Waeppa). Wappenbury Hall was the home of Sir William Lyons of Jaguar fame. Cross the fields to Princethorpe with fine views of Princethorpe College in the distance. It was built at the end of the 19th century using clay dug from the site for the bricks.

Cross the main road and join the Coffin Walk, restored by the local Scout Group, between **Princethorpe** (*Prandestorpe* in 1221, farmstead or a hamlet of a man called Praen or Pren old English) and the parish church at **Stretton on Dunsmore** (*Stratone* in the DB, farmstead or village on a Roman Road. *Dunesmore* 12th century is an old name meaning moor of a man called Dunn). This route veers right to enter the village at the rear of The Shoulder of Mutton, the oldest public house in the village.

Stretton on Dunsmore lies next to the Fosse Way and is thought to be of Anglo Saxon origin. A small brook runs through the village across its attractive green. A plastic duck race is held here annually in December, a maypole ceremony in May and morris-dancing at Whitsun. The most prominent black and white building by the green is Moor Farm. Although extended over the centuries, this played an important role in the village and is said to have been the location for the Manor Court.

The other public house, The Oak and Black Dog, was once just a terrace of three hundred year old cottages. The A45 north of the village hides the remains of the London to Holyhead road. Such was the importance of the road that the village once supported nine inns to provide hospitality to travellers over wild Dunsmore Heath. Perhaps the most significant claim to fame is the ceremony that dates back over 800 years and is held on the village boundary with **Ryton on Dunsmore**, (*Rietone* in DB, usually a farm where Rye is grown, Dunsmore as above).

Representatives of villages in the "Knightlow Hundred" gather before sunrise on November the 11th on Knightlow Hill for the payment of Wroth Silver. As dawn breaks, pennies are cast into the hollow Knightlow Stone as payment to the Lord of the Hundred, currently the Duke of Buccleuch. Failure to pay led to a fine of a white bull. A substantial breakfast follows at a local hostelry. True to tradition clay pipes are offered for smoking after the loyal toast in rum and hot milk.

Turn up Church Hill past the old vicarage, now Stretton House, on the right. The present church of All Saints was consecrated in 1837. It was built on the site of the previous

Norman church. The Manor House that stands on the corner is a combination of three older cottages and replaces a medieval Manor House near the village green.

Leaving the road to cross the fields on your right up to Plott Lane, the fields here were known as Poors Plot and the revenue used to support the village poor. There are still a number of allotments in cultivation.

Cross Freeboard Lane and fields to **Ryton on Dunsmore**, passing ponds on the left of the A45 that were used to water steam lorries years ago. Over the A45 can be seen St Leonard's Church, part Norman. Turn through the village past the Blacksmith's Arms to join A Coventry Way along the Peugeot walkway. Cross the Oxford Road and skirt round an old sand and gravel quarry, now a private lake behind high fences.

Cross Bubbenhall from an easterly direction in the footsteps of a local resident's grandfather (the local shoemaker) who walked into Coventry to collect leather from the tanneries in Tanners Lane. See pages 38 and 39 for more details of **Bubbenhall**.

Wildlife

This walk encircles the largest area of semi-natural woodland in the county. Ryton Wood and Wappenbury Wood are both Warwickshire Wildlife Trust reserves but the area also includes Old Nun Wood, Bubbenhall Wood and Princethorpe Great Wood. All the woods are predominantly oak but species such as birch, holly and small leaved lime occur frequently.

The landscape of this area is described as Dunsmore Parkland although it is perhaps difficult to imagine Norman barons and nobles riding in hot pursuit of deer. Indeed, the fallow deer that can still be encountered in the area probably owe their presence to the Normans who first introduced them from mainland Europe to Britain.

Another non-native deer that occurs in large numbers within the woods is the muntjac. Introduced to Woburn Park in Bedfordshire from China, this species has spread considerably since their escape/release in the 1920s. About the size of a large dog, the deer is easily recognised by the erect, white triangular shaped tail, which is the last thing to be seen as the animal disappears into the undergrowth.

Muntjac

Note on care with wildlife:-
On Route A the path follows a ride in Wappenbury Wood that is very muddy. Ensure that you don't interfere with wildlife when you negotiate as dry a route as possible.

Main Walk

1. With back to old school go left 100m, thro' p/g (in f/g) on left. **Fwd** along road & thro' fenced quarry workings until near boundary of wood, x-bridge over conveyor. **Fwd**, wood on right to x-stile into enclosed path. **Fwd** to x-stile into wood. **Fwd** up thro' wood to its end. Carefully follow authorities waymark directions to reach old metal signpost. Hg-right to corner, x-stile on left, **Fwd** along enclosed path to end, x-stile on right. Fc-right, passing two pools **to** reach electric pole. **T/L**, hg-right to reach & go over f/b on right. **H/L** cross-field to x-stile in field corner. Hg-left for 100m, cross foot-bridge on left, **fwd** cross-field to wood boundary. **T/R**, wood on left, to corner just past entrance to wood. **Fwd**, away from wood on same line cross-field (large) down to road & field corner (aim for houses).

2. Cross road & walk towards Wappenbury. 150m after village sign & as road bears right go thro' f/g on left. Brick wall & then fc-right up to field corner. **T/R** thro' gate, **H/L** cross-field to corner. Thro' f/g, hg-left to end of large field. Over concrete s/b, thro' k/g to go over bridle track & **fwd** with hg-left to go thro' gate at end of field. Fc-left & follow round to right to go over f/b on left. **H/R** cross-field uphill, under OPL to an outward hedge corner on top of hill. Thro' k/g & **fwd** hg-right to road.

3. **T/R** down road on far pavement to junction with main road. **Fwd** over main road to go up Sheep Dip Lane. Where road turns right, **fwd**, thro' k/g to start Coffin Walk. **Fwd** fenced path, thro' k/g, hg-right to far end. Thro' k/g, **H/L** cross-field to hedge line, **T/R** hg-left & thro' k/g. **Fwd** along gravel drive passing house on right to go over farm track & thro' k/g ahead. **Fwd** cross-field to start of hedge, keep hg-left, over track, **fwd** along an enclosed green track. X-stile at end, stream on right, hg-left thro' k/g. **H/R**, cross-field to follow waymark directions across paddocks & over concrete bridge, **fwd** to enter car park at rear of Shoulder of Mutton. **Fwd** towards village centre. **T/L** up Church Hill, round left bend to next junction with minor road. (**Route A** see below).

4. **T/R** along road for 100m, x-stile on right, fc-right to go thro' gap in hedge, **fwd** hg-right, **V/L** to bypass silos & barn to cut across field corner & reach boundary hedge. **T/L**, hg-right to reach & go thro' k/g on right, **fwd** for 150m, **T/R** thro' hedge gap. **T/R** fc/hg-right to reach enclosed path, follow round left to gravel path. **T/R** down drive thro' f/g to road. Thro' p/g opposite, **V/R** cross-field to pick up fc-right to corner, round left, hg-right to x-stile onto road.

5. X-stile opposite, **H/L** cross-field to go thro' hedge gap in far corner. Hg-left, x-stiles over 6 fields to reach A45. **V/L**, over private road, keep on grass verge to reach pavement, **fwd** to road junction. **Look for suitable crossing point away from A45 junction to cross A445.** Return to pavement adjacent to A45. **Fwd** for 500m, **T/L** into High Street.

6. **T/L** down road for 300m, **T/R** into Warren Fields, **T/L** to end of cul-de-sac. **T/R** thro' k/g into enclosed path. At junction of paths follow round to your left, & **fwd** to **busy** main road. Cross over to oppo-site pavement. **T/L** for 50m to x-stile on your right.

7. **H/L** cross-field into enclosed path. Follow round, left & right over stream bridge. **Fwd** hg-right, & then follow round right to farm track. **Fwd** along track hg-right/fc left. **T/L** at WMP & continue in same direction to Bubbenhall (Lower End). Up road to junction, **T/L** & then fork left to main road. The old school is along the road to your right.

Route A

At end of Note 3 **T/R** along road for 500m. X-stile on left, **fwd** cross-field to pick up hg-left. **Fwd** thro' wood, hg-left to **busy** main road. Opposite x-stile, hg-left over 2 fields to road. **Fwd** up road (1.2 km) to T-junction. **T/R**, wood left, at gate (Shady Acres), **T/R** along track to where it bends left just before entering Nature Reserve. **Fwd** leaving track to enter wood on path. After 400m thro' p/g into hedged path, **fwd** along to road/drive junc-tion. Down road left to junction, **T/R** for 1.2 km to main road. **T/L** to old school.

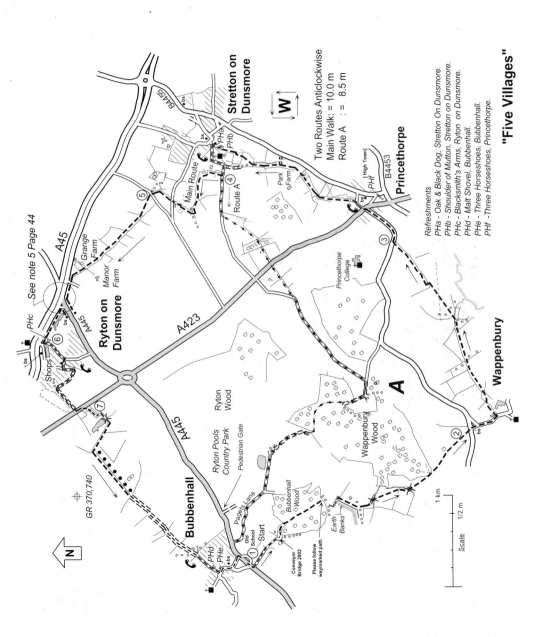

Two Routes Anticlockwise
Main Walk: = 10.0 m
Route A   : = 8.5 m

"Five Villages"

Refreshments
PHa - Oak & Black Dog, Stretton On Dunsmore.
PHb - Shoulder of Mutton, Stretton on Dunsmore.
PHc - Blacksmith's Arms, Ryton on Dunsmore.
PHd - Malt Shovel, Bubbenhall.
PHe - Three Horseshoes, Bubbenhall.
PHf - Three Horseshoes, Princethorpe.

Start : War Memorial,
Main Street, Wolston
Grid Ref. SP 412,756
Direction : Anticlockwise
Main Walk: = 9.0 miles
Route A : = 5.5 miles
OS Maps : (p = part)
: Landranger 140
: Pathfinder 955p
: Pathfinder 956p
: Explorer 221p
: Explorer 222p
Refreshments : (page 100
Oak & Black Dog
Stretton on Dunsmore
Shoulder of Mutton
Stretton on Dunsmore
Blacksmith's Arms
Ryton on Dunsmore
Rose & Crown   Wolston
Red Lion   Wolston
Half Moon   Wolston
Fish and Chips at Wolston
Pub. Transport : (a page 101
Start X86 & 86.
On or near route 538, 570 &
580.
Parking : Carefully in streets
adjacent to start.

Snippets:-
This is a grand tour from
Wolston to Ryton on
Dunsmore and Stretton on
Dunsmore & back using the
old village paths. It is
unfortunate that the A45
crosses the walk but the stiles
leading to the A45 are there
as well as gaps in the
reservation barriers (2002). It
is up to you to decide See
Traffic Notes on page 9.
There are some boggy parts
on the high ground but the
views are splendid.

It is important to remember with this walk that both the main route and Route A cross the A45, a fast dual carriageway, and the A45 / A445 junction. See Traffic Notes on page 9

Brief Information and Outline of Route

This walk starts at **Wolston** (*Ulvricetone* in the DB, farm or village of a man called Wulfric) near the war memorial.

The War Memorial and Old Post Office - Wolston

Kevin Wilkins

Go through the walkway past the school then skirt the wood where snowdrops can be seen in early spring and two millstones were found after being abandoned from an old mill in the area. The parish council hope to use them as part of a Millennium feature on the village green.

Glimpses of St Margaret's Church, part Norman, can be caught back across the meadow beside the Avon. Past the old school grounds and sewage works. On the opposite bank of the River Avon, now a golf course, is the site of an old Silk Mill. It closed at the end of the 19th century and fell into disrepair.

Up to the A45 and along to the subway near St Leonard's Church, part Norman, in **Ryton on Dunsmore**.

Back along the A45 past ponds where steam lorries filled up years ago. South east by Grange Farm and head across the fields to skirt the north of **Stretton on Dunsmore** (see page 42). Cross the Fosse Way east to Limekiln Farm then north of the A45 and through the Holdings, a small wood with fishing pools.

Across to Manor Farm and Hill Top Cottage across the Fosse again and back down to **Wolston**, past its cemetery.

Blacksmith's Arms - Ryton on Dunsmore

Kevin Wilkins

Wildlife

Don't let the name Dunsmore Heath confuse you. Up until the 18th century the area probably included extensive areas of heathland containing species such as heather and gorse. But since that time the land has been divided by hedgerows, grazed by sheep that would have removed heather and eventually gorse, and in more recent times ploughed as arable land. However, there remains a sense of exposure about the Dunsmore area as if roads and hedgerows have just been draped across the landscape rather than being an integral part of it.

It doesn't take a great deal of imagination to conjure up the impression of a windswept moor. Indeed, the lack of woodland in the area is a feature of the landscape rather than an omission and Dunsmore Heath would have been one of the earliest areas in Warwickshire where our ancient ancestors cleared the land of trees.

Another feature of the area is the deep sided pools that are found throughout much of Dunsmore, that appear to have been dug through the surface geology of well drained sands and gravels into the glacial clays below.

A long snippet:-

The first booklet on A Coventry Way was published in 1995. Its first draft had "A 35 Mile Circular Walk" title printed on the cover. Bob Watson, after walking it, settled down to a serious measure and came up with 39.70 miles, using 6in to the mile maps. Delighted, we settled for 40 and forgot about it. Some questions were asked when Ralph Chaplin ran round in 6 hours as it was a significant chunk off the previous best time. More serious questions were asked when Colin Kirkham put up the magnificent time of 5 hours 22 minutes and I think Colin himself thought it was around 38.5 miles. The task was clear, a measuring wheel was hired and in three days it was pushed round by three 'A Coventry Way Association' members. The wheel was regularly cleaned and a strict routine was followed of wheeling up to and re-starting from the centre line of stiles etc. Answer 40.09 miles. You may ask, what is this to do with Wolston? The Wolston War Memorial, for a very good reason, was where the measuring started and finished!

Main Walk (Do not take any risks, read Traffic Notes on page 9)

1. Walk towards church along drive past gate-house on left and then after 30m **T/L** up walkway, **fwd**, passing end of cul-de-sacs with wood on "near" right for approx. 500m. **T/R** at end into walkway that goes around the perimeter of sports field to field. **V/L** cross-field to go over farm drive ahead. **Fwd** cross-field to go thro' gap, cross-field to a further gap in corner. Cross-field to pick up hg-left to enter fenced walkway adjacent to Sewage Works, **fwd** to go over works drive at entrance. **H/R** cross-field to f/b & on similar line cross-field to next f/b. **Fwd**, uphill, h/g left, & then down to gap & descend steps to A45. **T/R** along pavement to subway.

2. Thro' subway to shops, carefully cross road to War Memorial. **Look for suitable crossing point away from A45 junction to cross A445, fwd** on pavement & wide verge adjacent to A45. Over private road to x-stile just inset on right. With hg-right, over stiles of fields ahead until hedgerow, with lane on other side, is reached. **T/L,** hg-right for 100m to exit field over stile onto road. (**Route A** see below).

3. Opposite x-stile on left of gate, **fwd** cross-field to go thro' gap on left of building ahead. **V/L** cross-field, x-stile, **fwd** cross-field to x-stile into walkway between school grounds on left & houses on right. Over school ground entrance to next road. **Fwd** over road, thro' gate & walkway between houses, thro' k/g & along closed field path to x-stile. **T/R,** thro' k/g along walkway to road (note for pubs & centre of village **T/R**).

4. **T/L** up road to junction, cross over road & go thro' recreation ground with boundary on left to far corner. At wooden fence, x-stile & **fwd** into field 15m ahead. **T/R,** hg-right & at corner **T/L** keeping hg-right for 250m to go over s/b on right. X-stile, hg-left to x-stile onto road. **T/R** for 200m to enter bridleway on left, **fwd** & then go downhill to p/g at end. Hg-left to pick up rough farm track ahead. **Fwd** on farm track until T-junction. **T/L** up track past farm buildings on right to A45. At boundary with A45 x-stile.

Cross A45 with great care

5. At lay-by go thro' gate (WMP), with hg-right **fwd** to **T/R** & **T/L** thro' gap. Fwd hg-left & bear round right to **T/L** into copse. **Fwd** on main path until it bends right, leave at WMP to follow narrow staked path through copse to corner. Over f/b on left, **H/R** cross-field to go up & x-stile next to gate in top hedge (pool). **T/R,**   hg-right to go thro' metal gate. **T/L,** hg-left to field corner, **T/R**   fc-left to farm track. **T/L** thro' metal gate, hg-right along farm track. **Fwd** hg-right over four fields until reaching & crossing a "double stile" with s/b. Cross-field to s/b & metal p/g. Cross-field to go thro' f/g ahead onto road.

6. **T/L** up road past Heath House & Business Park for 420m where road bends slightly right. **T/L** thro' f/g on left at end of cottage garden, **T/R** hg-right. X-stile off field corner, **V/L** cross-field (large), keeping on broad ridge, pool 60m on right to x-double stile and s/b in hedge ahead. **V/R,** aiming for left pair of "two pairs" of trees ahead to x-stile onto road.

7. X-stile just to right on opposite side, up hg-right, f/c right (passing two redundant stiles) to cross stile at top on right, with isolated tree in front. **T/L,** fc-left down to go over s/b and thro' k/g in hedge just off field corner. **V/R** cross-field to go thro' k/g onto road at corner of field. **T/R** down road past cemetery on right to main road. **T/L** & **T/R** to War Memorial.

Route A (Note that this route also involves crossing the A45).

At the end Note 2, **T/L** along road to A45. **Cross with great care.** X-stile up on left of cottage & keep hg-right up to x-stile and round until hedge turns sharp right. **V/L** cross-field aiming for right hand of hedge end (WMP). **Fwd** cross-field (roughly parallel to road on right) to hedge opposite. Over f/b, x-stile. **H/L** cross-field to x-stile into dell, **fwd** with pond on right to x-stile. **Fwd,** gradually down, cross-field to reach & x-stile onto road. **T/L** down to main road. **T/R** along road & **T/L** down Main Street to War Memorial.

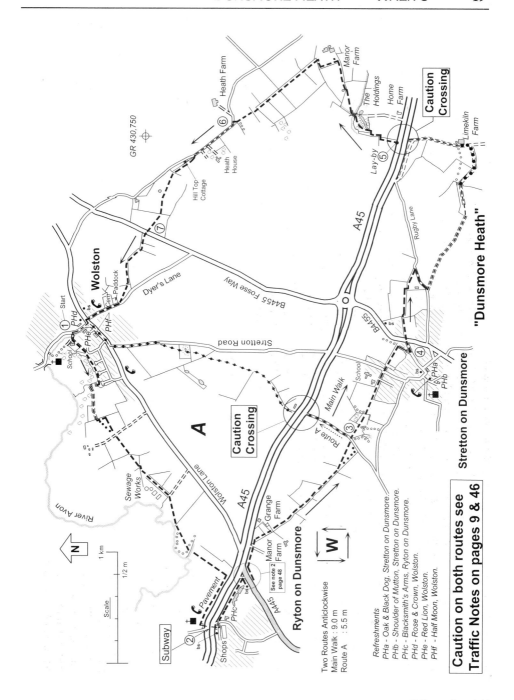

GR 430,750

Heath Farm

Manor Farm

The Holdings

Home Farm

Caution Crossing

Limekiln Farm

Heath House

Lay-by ⑤

Hill Top Cottage

⑥

⑦

A45

Rugby Lane

Wolston

Start

Paddock

Dyer's Lane

Cem

PHd

PHe

PHf

School

B4455 Fosse Way

①

"Dunsmore Heath"

Stretton Road

Main Walk

School

④

PHa

PHb

③

A

Caution Crossing

Route A

bs

Stretton on Dunsmore

Sewage Works

Wolston Lane

River Avon

A45

Grange Farm

Manor Farm

See note 2 page 48

W

Ryton on Dunsmore

Subway

②

Pavement

A45

PHc

Shops

bs

N

1 km

1/2 m

Scale

Two Routes Anticlockwise
Main Walk : 9.0 m
Route A : 5.5 m

Refreshments
PHa - Oak & Black Dog, Stretton on Dunsmore.
PHb - Shoulder of Mutton, Stretton on Dunsmore.
PHc - Blacksmith's Arms, Ryton on Dunsmore.
PHd - Rose & Crown, Wolston.
PHe - Red Lion, Wolston.
PHf - Half Moon, Wolston.

**Caution on both routes see
Traffic Notes on pages 9 & 46**

5/6/10 short

Start : *Priory Road, Wolston*
Grid Ref. SP 416,758
Direction : Anticlockwise
Main Walk: = 8.5 miles
Route A : = 5.5 miles
OS Maps : Landranger 140
: Pathfinder 956
: Explorer 222
Refreshments : ℓ page 100
The Old Smithy, Ch Lawford
The Queen's Head, Bretford
PHs in Brinklow page 58
PHs in Wolston page 46
Pub. Transport : ℓ page 101
Start X86 & 86. On or near route 585.
Parking : Carefully in streets adjacent to start.

Snippets:-
The ponds at King's Newnham, according to local knowledge, were drained by pulling the plug out of the lower pool to catch the fish.

Brief Information and Outline of Route

This walk starts outside **Wolston Priory** (see page 46), chiefly Elizabethan though it still has some stones of a priory founded in Norman times. It has a Tudor doorway with a massive old door and a cellar where a company of printers was working in Elizabeth I days.

Across fields east and north at the back of Limestone Hall, built of limestone locally quarried possibly in the 18th century. At one time limestone was extensively worked in the surrounding area. The workings gave rise to the discovery of the fossilised remains of many prehistoric animals.

So on to **Church Lawford** (*Lelleford* in the DB, *Chirche Lalleford* in 1235, ford of a man called Lealla). In the centre of the village at the Green is The Old Smithy public house, once known as The White Lion. Around the walls inside are many old photos of the village and sales documents of the building when it was sold by the Duke of Buccleuch's estate between the wars and many other interesting documents. In what were the stables there is now "Frankton - Bagby Micro - Brewery" brewing real ale, some of which can be bought in The Old Smithy.

In Green Lane can be found the last surviving thatched cottages in the village. Opposite The Old Smithy is the Reading Room, built in 1912, it now serves as the village hall. The Rectory down the main road, formally the residence of the incumbent of St Peter's Church, is now a private house.

The walk goes down Church Road towards St Peter's Church overlooking the River Avon. It was built in 1874 around a former 14th century church, parts of which can still be seen. Adjacent to the church stands the Elizabethan manor house, possibly the oldest complete building in the village.

Walk down the fields to cross the footbridge over the Avon into **King's Newnham**, (*Niwe* old English, the new homestead or enclosure) where there are remains of a water mill. Parts of the machinery and sluices can still be seen. A substantial part of the structure remained until the 1950s. A fire, however, began the decline. A mill mentioned in the DB was probably on the same site. Walkers are urged not to enter the site as it is private property.

Now into King's Newnham via a footpath between the topmost ponds. The ponds were created by the monks of Kenilworth to breed fish for food. The ponds are still used by members of an angling club. King's Newnham was included in the Manor of *Leileforde* in the DB, but in the reign of HenryII it became a parish in its own right. Across

Ruins of Mill at King's Newnham

Kevin Wilkins

the road is a fine 18ᵗʰ century house, King's Newnham Hall. In the grounds is a church tower, the remains of St Lawrence's Church last used in 1730. In 1852 six lead lined coffins were found, these were the remains of Francis, Earl of Chichester and his family, plus the remains of a headless man. He is thought to have been a Royalist sympathiser who was beheaded at the same time as Charles I.

Cross the field to skirt the south of **Brinklow** (see page 58) and down Tutbury Lane, an ancient "holloway" which may have linked Bronze and Iron age fields and farms before the Romans built the Fosse Way to reach **Bretford** (early 11ᵗʰ century, probably meaning a ford provided with planks). Bretford Villa, a redbrick house, was the village shop in the early 20ᵗʰ century. The Queen's Head was known as the "Friendly Inn" in 1848 and now incorporates what were separate small cottages. During sewage works in 1989 dozens of old shoes (including a Tudor one, now in Warwick Museum) were unearthed in front of Ivy Cottage Farm, occupied at the turn of the 19ᵗʰ century by a family of horse-breakers. But Bretford's hey-day was in the early Middle Ages. A long thin garden of the 15ᵗʰ century "Olde Oaks" is probably one of the original plots laid out for the Burgesses of this "town" which failed to develop. In the 12ᵗʰ century a small group of nuns settled here. There was also a leper hospital, its chapel continuing for another 200 years. Bretford Bridge is 18ᵗʰ century, replacing an earlier bridge first mentioned in 1279 and badly damaged in the Civil War. To the left of the bridge can be seen the old route of the Fosse Way as a holloway in the fields leading to a ford across the Avon. Marston Mill in the fields between Bretford and Wolston is now a farm on the site of a deserted village. The mill itself, now gone, may date from Domesday and could be the 12ᵗʰ century mill of Coombe Abbey, commanding the land given to Noemi the nun to support the cell at Bretford. Under the railway and back to **Wolston Priory**.

Wildlife

Still within the Dunsmore Heath area the peculiar nature of the underlying geology has added a further dimension of wildlife interest. The acidic layers of sand, gravel and clay typical of the Dunsmore Heath here overlay calcareous Lias layers, which are limestone rocks and clay from the Jurassic period. Over time the River Avon and its myriad of small streams and tributaries have dissected the upper glacial material to reveal the older rocks. Old buildings in the area often include walls of soft limestone blocks and have names with terms such as Limekiln and Limestone.

Woodland occurs in the area but only as small relatively isolated patches in the southern extent of the walk such as Dingley Osier, The Thicket and Fulham Wood. The latter of these is an elm woodland, which suffered greatly as a result of Dutch Elm Disease. The others were probably part of an old basket making industry, but the area is no longer fed by the adjacent ditch, and trees such as oak are the most common here. In the north the much larger All Oaks Wood is no longer true to its name in that the most abundant tree is ash. The ground flora reflects in places the wet conditions that prevail in the wood with species such as sweet woodruff, yellow pimpernel, ragged robin and bugle being the more interesting finds.

Grassland habitats are largely confined to the village fringes and include an area east of Church Lawford that is privately owned and managed largely for nature conservation benefit. Although species such as ox-eye daisy, pignut, germander speedwell, meadow vetchling and buttercups are encountered at Church Lawford, Bretford and Brinklow, other species more indicative of the calcareous nature of the soil can be found and this includes greater knapweed, lady's bedstraw and meadow barley.

Walkers may wish to linger a while on the River Avon crossing north of Church Lawford. Bird life in this area is rich with warblers such as whitethroat and sedge warbler, nesting mute swan, the ubiquitous heron and the possibility of kingfisher. Summer visitors may also encounter the banded demoiselle, a large and most beautiful damselfly that has a curious association with common club-rush. The common club-rush with its dark olive green stems is a characteristic species of deep slow flowing rivers, the banded demoiselle relies on this species alone to allow the aquatic born larvae a pathway to the sky.

Main Walk

1. Opposite the Priory entrance go thro' k/g & **fwd** cross-field to go thro' a k/g to the right of far left corner onto road. **T/L** & shortly **T/R** up road (Coalpit Lane) **fwd** over <u>main road</u>, up minor

road ahead then as it bears right (pole DP 408) WMP x-stile on left and then x-stile on right. **H/L** <u>plus</u> cross-field, x-stile left of Ash tree, **V/R** cross-field, parallel to road hedge on right. Thro' "smallest" hedge gap, immediately x-stile on right, **T/L**, fc-left. X-stile in fence ahead & **fwd** hg-left to field corner. Over stiles & bridge, keep hg-right to field corner over f/b, **fwd** hg-right, to a f/b on right, **do not go over**, **H/L** cross-field to right end of wood. Over bridge & x-stile, cross-field up past a slurry pit on your right, aim just left of farm wall to gain minor road.

Wolston Priory

2. **T/L** down road for 120m & at WMP **V/R** cross-field to x-stiles & steps ahead. Hg-right for 250m to x-double stile ahead. **Fwd** cross-field <u>leaving</u> hg-left, aim for right corner, over bridge, hg-right, x-stile on right in corner. **T/L**, hg-left to corner, x-stiles & bridge on left, **T/R**, hg-right to corner. X-stile, cross-field to gap in opposite hedge, **fwd** cross-field to go thro' f/g onto road.

3. **T/L** down road, over railway bridge to road junction, cross <u>main road</u> into School Street. **T/R** down road to church. With back to church, x-stile, **H/L** cross-field to far left corner. X-stile & shortly x-stile on right, **fwd** down enclosed path, over track, cross-field to x-stile in fence then long footbridge over River Avon. Thro' mill ruins, **H/L** uphill, to reach and to go between top two fish ponds. Exit onto road thro' p/g. (**Route A** see below).

4. **T/R** up to junction, **T/L** & immediately **T/R** thro' f/g. Up track with hg-right **fwd** up to pass end of wood on left. **H/L** cross-field to gap in hedge. **Fwd** on same line cross-field to s/b & x-stile, cross-field to go over f/b ahead. **H/R** to x-stile onto road.

5. Thro' p/g (in f/g) opposite, **H/L** cross-field. At right hand end of small copse, **fwd** cross-field to far left corner of wood ahead. Over s/b, keep wood on right for 50m, then **T/L** thro/ h/g & over s/b & x-stile. **H/R** to reach double f/gs in hedge ahead, x-stile on left of two f/gs, **fwd** hg-right to x-stile in corner. **H/R** cross-field to meet hedge on right just after f/g. **Fwd** hg-right to x-stile right of gate. **Fwd** cross-field to far corner, x-stile onto main road.

6. **Fwd** along main road into Brinklow, pass Broad St on right, shortly & before Heath Lane **T/L** at WMP into enclosed path behind gardens. Just <u>before</u> stile **T/L**, hg-right, **T/R** thro' f/g at end of field onto road. Immediately **T/L** up bridle track, continue forward at junctions & go down into Bretford.

7. At road **fwd**, over river to road junction. **Fwd** across road (**with care**) thro' p/g opposite, **T/R**, hg-right to exit field thro' k/g in corner. **Fwd** across road (**with care**) into drive opposite, go thro' k/g on right at end of drive. Fc-left & then bank left, **fwd** over two fields fc-left to reach farm buildings. **Fwd** in front of barn, **T/R**, & shortly **T/L** on farm track, **fwd** over cattle grid, under railway tunnel & then along road to return to the start.

Route A

At the end of Note 3 **T/R** up to junction, **T/L** and walk along minor road to Bretford. After joining the main road at Bretford, **fwd** past The Queen's Head. At junction keep left to traffic lights, continue with Note 7.

Nicola Bean

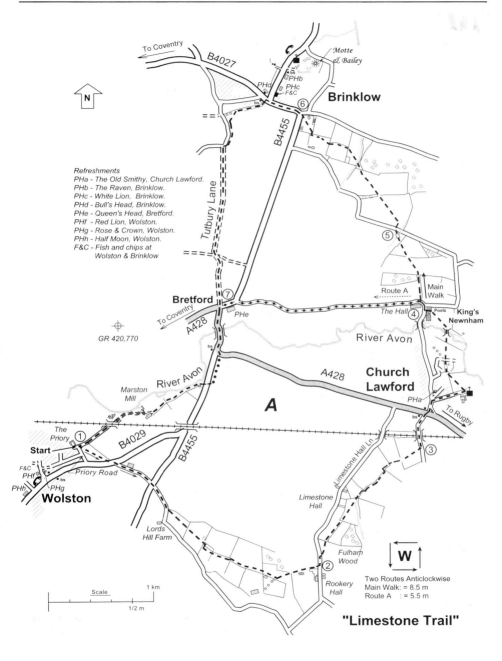

Refreshments
PHa - The Old Smithy, Church Lawford.
PHb - The Raven, Brinklow.
PHc - White Lion, Brinklow.
PHd - Bull's Head, Brinklow.
PHe - Queen's Head, Bretford.
PHf - Red Lion, Wolston.
PHg - Rose & Crown, Wolston.
PHh - Half Moon, Wolston.
F&C - Fish and chips at
        Wolston & Brinklow.

Two Routes Anticlockwise
Main Walk = 8.5 m
Route A   : = 5.5 m

"Limestone Trail"

Start : Coombe Abbey
    Visitor Centre.
Grid Ref. SP 403,795
Direction : Clockwise
Main Walk: = 9.0 miles
Route A : = 6.5 miles
OS Maps : Landranger 140
         : Pathfinder 956
         : Explorer   222
Refreshments : (page 100
Royal Oak, Brandon.
Coombe Country Park,
Cafeteria.
PHs in Brinklow   page 58
PHs in Wolston   page 46
PH in Bretford   page 50
Pub. Transport : (page 101
Start 585.
On or near route X86 & 86.
Parking : Car park near
visitor centre (charge).

Snippets:-

A New Discovery Centre has
been opened in 2002. It is
totally interactive with spy
holes to peep through, things
to feel and hear, games to play
and information to read. For
further details contact Coombe
Country Park on:-
024 7645 3720

In 1603 Elizabeth, the
daughter of James I, came to
live and be educated at
Coombe Abbey. In 1605, Guy
Fawkes's Gunpowder Plot
failed. His plan had been to
kidnap Elizabeth from Coombe
Abbey and put her on the
throne. Later she married
King Frederick V and became
known as the "Winter Queen
of Bohemia". She had 13
children, 8 boys and 5 girls.

The corrugated enclosure at
Brandon is currently the home
of The Coventry Bees
Speedway.

Brief Information and Outline of Route

This walk starts at Coombe Abbey visitor centre. The Abbey (*Abbey of Cumbe* as it was known in the 12th century) was founded by Cistercian monks, then it was acquired by John Harrington who built a new house around the abbey. The Craven family bought the Abbey in the 17th century and it remained in their care for the next 300 years. In the 18th century Lancelot "Capability" Brown redesigned the gardens and the surrounding land. In 1922 the estate was divided into 166 lots and sold by the family. Through the first part of the 20th century Coventry City Council gradually acquired land and then in 1964 the Abbey itself. Coombe Abbey Regional Park was opened to the public in 1966. In 1993 the new visitor centre, events field and playground were opened.

Past the Rolls Royce plant and up the lane to Peter Hall where it is said that the remains of St Peter's Church can be found.

Over Smite Brook and across the fields to **Brinklow** (see page 58).

From Brinklow southward to **Brandon** (*Brandune* in DB, hill where broom grows) with its important 12th century *Motte and Bailey* castle of the Verdons surrounded by Moat and Pools which would have been controlled by sluices. The remains of Brandon and Wolston station (LMS line) are still easily visible opposite the Royal Oak and would have served Brandon House (now Brandon Hall). A 19th century house with a large ruined kitchen garden some distance away.

Nearby and towards Coventry is Brandon Wood, with an impressive medieval double ditch, given by the Forestry Commission to be managed by local friends as a community woodland.

Past the speedway stadium and down the Twelve O'Clock Ride (named by its position to the noon day sun) and back to Coombe Abbey for a well deserved cuppa.

Possible Short Cut

If you do not want to continue towards Brandon there is a diversion on the Main Walk. You will miss the good views as you descend but also the bridleway that can be muddy! At the end of Note 5 (page 56) continue **fwd** on bridleway to junction in Note 7 line 6. Continue with rest of note 7.

Wildlife

The Twelve O'Clock Ride is the name of the track that runs in a straight line from the eastern edge of Brandon Village following magnetic north all the way to Coombe Abbey. The path passes through the heart of New Close Wood, which is predominately oak woodland with ash and frequent silver birch. Other woody species to look out for include hazel, holly, rowan, aspen, field maple and elm. Honeysuckle is generally quite frequent with its tangle of fraying stems creating a lacework of twisted branches between closely growing trees and shrubs. The ground flora is equally interesting with bluebell, wood anemone, wood sorrel, foxglove, lords and ladies, greater stitchwort, herb robert, wood avens, skull cap, enchanter's nightshade, red campion and an array of fern tussocks.

Access to Coombe Park is free and, with its large ribbon lake and semi-natural woodland fringe, care of Capability Brown, is definitely worth a visit. The park is a Site of Special Scientific Interest on account of its impressive bird populations, which includes the largest heronry in the country.

On approaching the B4029 you'd be forgiven for thinking that you were nearing an extensive area of woodland. However, what you have encountered is a wooded fringe of approximately 100 metres in width that runs along the edge of the B4029 and B4027. It is assumed that the wood was planted as a shelterbelt to keep stock safe from stormy weather but that land is now used for arable production.

Heron

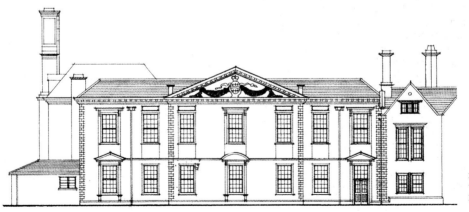

Coombe Abbey West Side

Mark Hampson

Main Walk Thro' the park a permissive path is followed, look for white arrows on green background

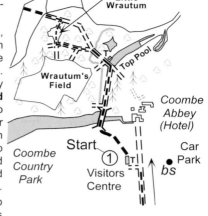

1. With your back to the rear of Visitor Centre, (north end), **V/L** along path to cross main bridge, over Coombe Lake. **Fwd** with Smite Brook left to Top Pool and Toilets on right. **Fwd** over bridge with metal railings. Shortly take left junction, after 200m **T/R** into and **fwd** cross open space (Little Wrautum). **Fwd** to path junction, **T/L** to Park boundary. Exit over s/b and thro' fence gap, cross-field to gap in hedge ahead. **Fwd** hg-right to go thro' k/g to farm track. **T/R** & follow track round right and left (thro' farmyard) to road. **T/L** up road and shortly **T/R**, after farm (WMP) thro' f/g on right.

2. **H/L** cross-field, take sighting from waymark to gate gap in fence. Aim cross-field towards farm buildings to go over bridge. Thro' p/g, **V/L** to field corner at junction of farm drive and road, over fence onto road. **T/R** along road for 275m to the end of houses, at the top of 'no thro' road x-stile on right.

3. **V/L** cross-field to go thro' k/g in opposite corner. **H/R**, close to hg-right to x-stile in opposite corner (path junction). **Fwd** hg-left, thro' k/g on left just before field boundary. **H/R** cross-field to far right hand corner to go thro' k/g onto track, **fwd** up track & then road to main road. **T/R** to junction, **T/R** & shortly enter walkway (WMP) on opposite side. **Fwd** along walkway behind houses to stile (do not cross).   (**Route A** see below).

4. **T/L**, hg-right to go thro' f/g on right at end of field. **T/L** (WMP) & go up hedged bridleway for approx 1km to bridleway crossroads.

5. **T/R** & follow this bridleway for approx. 750m, thro' gap on left of f/g just before junction, keep **fwd** for a further 500m, ignoring p/g to bridleway on left that turns sharply back.

6. **T/L** at gap with waymark on fence post & go down hedge/fenced bridleway, continue as it bends right, thro' p/g hg-right to road.

7. At this point do not enter road, **T/R** thro' large gates & aim up cross-field for right of house far ahead. Pass hedged pool on left to pick up hgh-left, 60m right of house. (WMP) **Fwd** hg-left to x-stile onto track. **Fwd** over track to go thro' gates & up drive, corrugated fence on left. Pass pond on left, do not enter properties ahead. At start of drive to house on left **T/L** alongside concrete garage to large oak tree. **T/R**, corrugated fence left to go over s/b to track. **T/L** along track to junction. **T/L** along drive (ignore p/g into paddock). After 240 metres enter Twelve O'clock Ride thro' p/g on right.

8. **Fwd** along ride thro' wood & then fields to cross over **busy** main road.

9. Enter park, **fwd** up drive & finish at car park

Route A (Note quarrying in this area so follow waymark directions) At the end of Note 3, x-stile & go over road into gravel drive (WMP). At the end of the drive with bungalow on left, **fwd** over green path for a short distance to its end. X-stile on left, **H/R** to cross-field, aim for opposite corner, oak tree, 40m up from corner go over s/b & thro hedge gap. Cross-field parallel to hedge on left to join quarry road at entrance. Thro' entrance & immediately **T/R**, hg-right, initially bank left to go thro' hedge gap at field corner. **Fwd** hg-right to track at wood boundary. **T/R** up track to road, **T/L** along **busy** main road for approx. 600m to park entrance. Continue with Note 9.

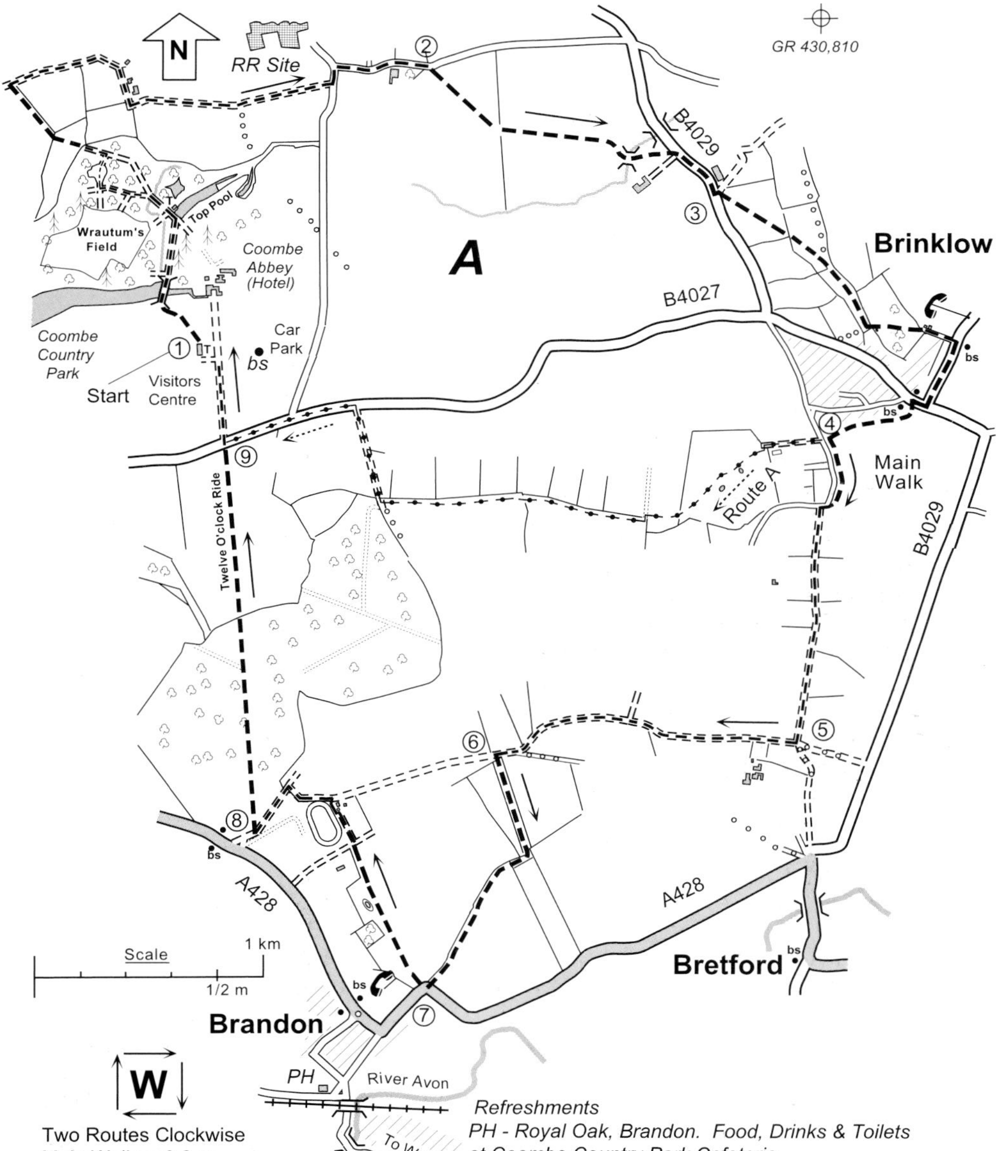

N

RR Site

GR 430,810

Brinklow

B4029

③

B4027

A

Wrautum's Field

Top Pool

Coombe Abbey (Hotel)

Coombe Country Park

Car Park
bs

Visitors Centre

Start

①

②

bs

Twelve O'clock Ride

⑨

Route A

Main Walk

④

B4029

⑥

⑤

⑧

bs

A428

A428

Bretford

bs

Brandon

bs

⑦

Scale

1 km

1/2 m

W

Two Routes Clockwise
Main Walk: = 9.0 m
Route A   : = 6.5 m

PH

River Avon

To Wolston

Refreshments
PH - Royal Oak, Brandon. Food, Drinks & Toilets
at Coombe Country Park Cafeteria.
See also Walks 9, 10 and 12 for other refreshment
outlets at Wolston, Bretford & Brinklow.

"The Abbey"

17|4|10

Start : Barr Lane, off Broad Street, Brinklow.
Grid Ref. SP 434,796
Direction : Clockwise
Main Walk: = 8.5 miles
Route A : = 7.0 miles
OS Maps : (p = part)
**   : Landranger 140**
**   : Pathfinder 956p**
**   : Pathfinder 936p**
**   : Explorer   222**
Refreshments : (page 100
All in Brinklow
The Raven
The White Lion
The Bull's Head
Fish & Chips
Chinese Take Away
Pub. Transport : (page 101
Start 585.
Parking : Carefully in car parking area or street.

Snippets:- *On Route A you pass under Brinklow Arches. This was Brindley's largest aqueduct in terms of height combined with length. There were twelve arches, each with a 22ft. span, the highest being 31ft. 6ins. The whole structure was 300 ft. long, connected to a 600 ft. embankment at one end and 400 ft. at the other. It is only possible to see one complete arch today, the one over the Smite Brook. Beside it is the original top of the second arch. One side of the aqueduct was filled in, in order to widen the channel, which used to be wide enough for only one boat. The other side has gradually been filled in with dredging.*
Note on the east side of the aqueduct, in spring time, is a splendid bank of cowslips.

Brief Information and Outline of Route

This walk starts at **Brinklow**. Its name is thought to have originated from the old English *Brynca-hlaw*, burial mound of a man called Brynca or on the brink of a hill. The village's most notable feature is the *Motte & Bailey* known locally as "The Tump". At the foot of "The Tump" is the church of St John the Baptist, built around 1252 by the Augustin Canons of Kenilworth Priory. The Oxford Canal, open by 1794, used to contour through Brinklow. It was never truly competitive as it took the whole day to go through the village, crossing the main road twice. Once between where Carlton House now stands and the iron gates opposite. Then behind The Crescent and Broad Street and again back through Dock Yard.

A more direct route was opened in 1834, by that date Brinklow had lost its "through canal". The only parts left with water can be seen from the footpath (ACW) from "The Tump" down to the corner of the main road leading to Bretford and the Brinklow Arm just south of the cemetery.

There are many pubs in Brinklow, The White Lion being one of the earliest.

Cross the fields to walk over Pedlar's packhorse bridge, restored in the 19th century. The bridge is on the route of a bridle way leading from the deserted medieval village of Upper Smite to Brinklow.

Kevin Wilkins

Now on to Grimes Bridge and the Oxford Canal. This canal was started in 1769 and was completed to Oxford in 1790. The canal bed is lined with puddle, a mixture of the right kind of soil and water to make it impervious. This was often trampled for hours by the navvies to get the right consistency. Take the track up the bank and over the steel viaduct to Mobbs Wood. Past the trees on the right are the remains of the abandoned village of *Upper Smite*. The villagers were evicted by the monks of Coombe Abbey in 1150 to make way for sheep.

Cross the M6 and fields eastwards to **Stretton under Fosse**, (*Straet+Tun* old English, farmstead or village on a Roman road). Through the village and down the drive towards the gates of HM Prison College at Newbold Revel. Sir Thomas Mallory, author of Morte d'Arthur, lived in the old 15th century mansion. Sir Thomas died in Newgate Prison in 1470. The old house has gone and the present building was built in the early 18th century.

Across the railway and past the old orchard, cross the road to Town Thorns Farm, with its many containers full of flowers during the summer. Over the canal and follow the water back towards Brinklow. Leaving the canal at the next bridge to pass "The Tump" into the village where there is a wide choice of refreshments.

Wildlife

Another high summer walk with some interesting canal-side sections. Keep an eye open for herons fishing along the canal early in the morning. If you reduce your pace and go carefully you can get quite close to these impressive birds.

At Grimes Bridge you access the Oxford Canal containing marginal meadowsweet, buttercup, common vetch with water dock, tall emergent sedge and grasses, bush vetch, herb robert, meadow vetchling, wood avens, lady's smock and germander speedwell.

On passing under the M6 you encounter a particularly rich stretch of canal embankment. This area contains common and bush vetch, hogweed, birds foot trefoil, yarrow, field forget-me-not, meadow buttercup, hedge woundwort, black medick, germander speedwell and ground ivy. The area also includes small wet patches with rushes meadowsweet, wild angelica, meadow vetchling and creeping cinquefoil. However, perhaps the most interesting species is the giant horsetail. Much larger versions of this species are commonly found as fossilised remains within carboniferous limestone dating back over 300 million years. The whole embankment is heavy with invertebrate life during the height of summer and this attracts a wide variety of small song birds.

The wet meadow to the south of Mobbs Wood is also very rich with stands of reed, tussocks of rush and expanses of marsh horsetail, great willowherb with tall sedges, water figwort and brooklime. The drier parts include common vetch, buttercup, yarrow, lady's smock and field woodrush.

As you follow a small stream and hedge along side the prison college keep an eye open for marsh marigold. This impressively colourful early flowering plant has become quite rare because of past draining of wetlands and current ditch clearance work. Here it manages to hang on despite encroaching scrub along the banks of the brook.

Either side of the railway line you will encounter some small broad leaf plantations. In the north, a thin shelter belt contains horse chestnut and hawthorn, some dogs mercury, ground ivy and hedge woundwort. In the south, the woodlands are a mix of oak, birch, ash and hawthorn with a ground flora dominated by nettle.

On rejoining the Oxford Canal you will encounter a rich mix of grassland and wetland species including hogweed, common vetch, meadowsweet, buttercup, herb robert, white bryony, wild parsnip and water dock with tall emergent sedges and grasses.

On nearing the road you will discover a small community woodland. This may provide some welcome shelter on a warm summers day. If you care to wander along the network of paths you will find that it is an oak and ash woodland with hawthorn, field maple, hazel, willow and dog rose. The ground flora contains abundant tall wood brome with wood avens, bramble, sweet woodruff, wood millet, honeysuckle and bluebell.

Beyond the woodland exists a strip of vegetation between the canal and road. Here you with encounter a mixture of grassland and woodland species including hawthorn, common vetch, wood avens, sweet woodruff, herb robert, wood brome, ground ivy, hedge woundwort, lords and ladies, bugle and occasional common spotted orchid. Includes some wet features with tall tussock sedges, rushes and grasses and marsh thistle.

The end of the walk is marked by the Brinklow Motte and Bailey. Although not tremendously rich, the area does include pignut and burnet saxifrage, two interesting short grassland umbellifers (related to hogweed). If you have the energy, be sure to make your way to the top of the castle mound where you can look down upon some fine examples of ridge and furrow.

Main Walk

1. Where cart track starts at the end of Barr Lane **fwd** along track for 30m, thro' k/g on your left into field, cross-field, aim to pass two isolated trees on left, **fwd** to hedge-line. Thro' k/g on right of hedged pool, **T/R** & with hg-right continue to field corner & x-stile at side of gate. Take right path & keep hg-right to field corner. X-stile at side of gate, **fwd** with hg-right under OPL thro' k/g in corner. **V/R** along bridle track ahead, cross over Pedlar's Bridge to road.

2. **T/L** & then shortly **T/R** & up road to just before bridge over canal. **T/L** to gain access to canal towpath. Along towpath (canal right!) to go under M6 & then a metal bridge, after 70m climb up embankment turning back towards bridge to reach track.

3. **T/L** over bridge along track for 500m, when track curves right towards farm **V/L** to x-stile. Initially fc-left, then aim for far corner of pinewood on right, x-stile, **T/R**, thro' gate, **fwd** wood boundary on right. At end of wood go thro' short fenced path, **T/R** & then shortly **T/L**, hg-right to next field boundary. Thro' gap ahead **T/R** & then **T/L** hg-right. Just before next field boundary **T/R** thro' gap, hg-left follow **fwd** to road & go over motorway.

4. Immediately after bridge x-stile on left into enclosed path, continue to cross s/b & then **H/R** cross-field aiming for left of barn. At barn keep hg-right until it finishes. **H/L** downfield towards track with hedge coming in on left. Thro' large gap at field boundary & go over culvert. **Fwd** with hg-left to reach road. Straight over, with hg-left & then x-stile fc-right. **H/L** on cart track to reach & go thro' k/g, over cattle grid & **fwd** down to main road.

5. **T/L** along road & shortly **T/R**, down road to gate of HM Prison College. **T/R** along enclosed path then thro' f/g to road.
   (**Route A** see below).

6. **Fwd** in enclosed path opposite to join drive. Follow drive for a very short distance where it bears left go thro' f/g on right. **T/L** & aim for & go thro' "posted gap" in fence, cross-field slightly right to reach far right corner. Thro' gap, **H/L** cross-field to go over footbridge. **H/L** cross-field to reach right side of copse & x-stile in corner. Up field with copse left (ignore stile left) & **T/L** to go thro' gap between copse & old orchard. **T/R**, old orchard right, up to corner & thro' p/g. Over track, thro' p/g, cut across corner of field to meet drive thro' k/g. **T/L** down drive to cross road ahead.

7. **Fwd** down long drive & pass thro' farm buildings. Thro' k/g, **T/L** & go over canal bridge. Bear round right, at the end of the garage/outbuildings of canal house **T/R** thro' gap into field. Hg-right for a short distance thro' hedge gap to reach towpath. **T/L** along towpath, continue past car park/picnic site to first bridge over canal.

8. Up steps on approaching side of bridge to road, **T/L** along road to junction, x-stile opposite into field & **V/R** to pass between electricity poles to reach moat. Keep moat on right & follow round to x-stile in corner. **T/L** over stile, follow enclosed path to road. **T/L** & shortly **T/R** into Barr Lane & the car park.

Route A

At the end of Note 5 cross road, go thro' f/g on right. **T/R** and pick up path at stream side. Continue along path, stream left, under railway, and canal and thro' wood. **T/L** over bridge, **T/R**, stream right to reach main road. **T/L** along pavement into Brinklow and **T/R** into Barr Lane.

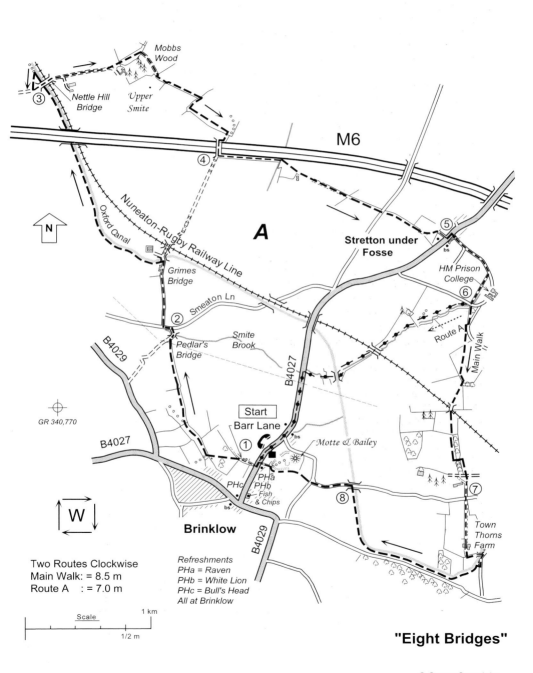

Mobbs Wood

Nettle Hill Bridge

③

Upper Smite

M6

④

N

Oxford Canal

Nuneaton-Rugby Railway Line

⑤

Stretton under Fosse

bs

HM Prison College

⑥

Grimes Bridge

A

Route A

Smeaton Ln

Main Walk

②

Pedlar's Bridge

Smite Brook

B4029

B4027

Start

Barr Lane

①

bs

Motte & Bailey

⑦

⑧

B4027

PHc

PHa

PHb

Fish & Chips

bs

Town Thorns Farm

W

GR 340,770

Brinklow

B4029

Two Routes Clockwise
Main Walk: = 8.5 m
Route A   : = 7.0 m

Refreshments
PHa = Raven
PHb = White Lion
PHc = Bull's Head
All at Brinklow

Scale

1 km

1/2 m

"Eight Bridges"

Start : Junction of Overstone Road & Featherbed Lane **Grid Ref. SP 435,846** **Direction : Clockwise** **Main Walk: = 7.5 miles** **Route A   : = 6.0 miles** **OS Maps : (p = part)** **   : Landranger 140** **   : Pathfinder   936p** **   : Pathfinder   935p** **   : Explorer   221p** **   : Explorer   222p** **Refreshments : (page 100** **The Pheasant, Withybrook.** **Rose & Castle, Ansty.** **Golf Club Restaurant, Ansty.** **The Shilton Arms, Shilton.** **Pub. Transport : (page 101** **Start** **From Rugby 222, 241 & 242** **On or near route 74&75** **Parking : Small hard standing at junction.**

Brief Information and Outline of Route

This walks starts at **Withybrook** (*Wythibroc* in the 12th century Willow-Tree Brook) originally a chapelry of Monks Kirby. The village lies on a tributary of the River Sowe. From the junction go down Overstone Road, the route leaves the road towards the church via a stile. Before crossing the stile look to the left where amongst the trees, and snowdrops in springtime, some 19th century tombstones can be found. We haven't been able to find out why they are isolated from the church grounds.

Over the meadow to All Saints Church, to the east of which is a field with some earthworks in. Back up Main Street pass The Pheasant and over the fields past Hopsford Spring to Hopsford Old Hall Farm with the site of an old village and manor house nearby.

Forward across the fields to a pool and evidence of the old Oxford contour canal that ran behind Hopsford Hall. Under Hopsford (*Apleford* in DB) Aqueduct and on to **Ansty** (*Anestie* in the DB, track linking other routes).

Cross the road opposite the Rose and Castle and down to the canal side. St James' Church is on the hill to the right. The spire was designed and built in Victorian times. The graves of six airmen who died in 1941 are in the churchyard. Beside the church is Ansty Hall, built in the 17th century and now a hotel. Under the M69 and right up to Barnacle Hall.

Kevin Wilkins

Barnacle Hall

Then east to skirt around **Shilton** (*Scelftone* in DB, farm on a ledge) with its St Andrew's Church. Through Shilton Lodge farm and back to Withybrook. In Withybrook at the junction of Featherbed Lane and Overstone Road is a young oak planted on the 50th anniversary of the victory in Europe May 8th 1995.

Wildlife

A summer walk which includes small wetland areas and old pasture. Worth taking a small pair of binoculars and spending a little time trying to spot small birds among tall wetland vegetation and low scrub. Also keep an eye open for butterflies. Brimstone and orange tip are generally common in the more wetland areas but meadow brown, ringlet and skippers are frequently encountered in and around the grasslands.

The first area of particular interest you will encounter is around Hopsford Springs. The ground here can be very moist and supports a wide variety of wetland plants including a number of tall grass and sedge species as well as a variety of rushes, great willowherb, water figwort and brooklime. This type of vegetation extends along the brook and is set in an area of old pasture. Keep your ears open for the distinctive sound of warblers that inhabit the area.

On the way from Hopsford Springs to Hopsford Hall you encounter some part wooded pools. A small fragment of meadow still remains in the area and supports species such as buttercups with the early flowering lesser celandine, and pignut. The pools are generally fringed with ash and hawthorn and contain willows at the water's edge. The area supports species such as lesser celandine, lords and ladies, ground ivy, red campion, wild angelica, meadowsweet and marsh marigold as well as tall sedges, reed and yellow iris along the wet banks of the pools and in shallows. The wetland character of the area continues on past the pools beyond which is a large open pool containing some wildfowl. Plenty of bird life in the area, occasionally visited by curlew, therefore it is advised to make a quiet approach on a warm still day.

Passing below the twin bridges for the railway line and canal you cannot help but feel that you have crossed through a gateway to another land. An expanse of grassland may be under threat from the nearby golf course. This is currently unmanaged grassland containing occasional lesser knapweed, goat's beard, rosebay willowherb, common vetch and hawkweeds. More wetland features are encountered along the canal which loops back on itself in this area and is encountered again beyond the golf course.

Beyond the M69 and once you have reached the country road you might wish to take a short break. Agrimony, lesser knapweed and goat's beard occur along the road verge and you may be lucky enough to find the former in flower with its tall spike of delicate yellow flowers.

Meadowsweet

Main Walk

1. Walk South down Overstone Road, just past start of pavement on left look for stile at top of bank on left. X-stile, cross-field down to church, thro' p/g to church yard & over bridge, **T/R** to Main St. & Pheasant.

2. **T/R** up Main Street for 200m, x-stiles on left, opposite Overstone Rd. Cross-field with its ups & downs, keeping parallel with hedge on left aiming for gate. Over culvert into next field, **fwd** cross the next two fields via culverts, cross & exit the next field via a s/b & x-stile near top right corner & then in 20m **T/R** over another s/b & x-stile. Thro' vegetation, **T/L**, then at ranch fence ahead thro' p/g, **T/L** to road thro' p/g.

3. **T/R** along road. **T/L** opp. farm & go thro' gap beside f/g. Go **fwd** cross-field towards hedgerow on far side. Look, and aim for tall WMP ahead. On reaching field boundary and WMP, with pools up on right, pass into next field, keep right, with hg/bank right follow round and over f/b. **Fwd** to vegetation & shallow bank right as it bears right, then **fwd** to meet lane. **T/L** down lane passing Hopsford Hall on right, follow on under the railway & then Hopsford Aqueduct. When lane turns left, **fwd** cross-field to outward hedge corner. **Fwd** keeping hg-right onto road. (**Route A** see below).

4. **T/R** up road for 20m, x-stile on left, next to gate, **fwd** cross-field to hedge opposite, **T/R**, hg-left, thro' k/g, up field to exit thro' k/g (right of gate). **Fwd** over canal bridge thro' p/g, up enclosed path to road. **T/L** down road, on pavement, to reach Rose & Castle.

5. X-stile opposite the Rose & Castle. **H/L** cross-field passing telegraph post to canal side. **Fwd** canal left, x-stile, thro' kg & under motorway bridge (M69). Exit thro' k/g, **T/R** & up to go thro' k/g in hedge ahead. Keep motorway right up into field corner. **T/L**, hg-right continue up to corner & x-stile just off field corner. **Fwd** hg-right, x-stile & s/b leading to road.

6. **T/L** & after 130m enter drive to Barnacle Hall & continue up drive to pass hall on right, across concrete yard. Thro' f/g ahead, aim for house opposite & skirt pool on your right to go thro' k/g to road.

7. **T/R** down road & when road turns right **fwd** thro' f/g on left of a pair. Hg-right to bottom right hand corner, thro' gap on right. **H/L** cross-field to opposite corner. X-stile into garden, keep conifer hedge right to go thro' p/g leading to farm track ahead. **T/R** along farm track & follow round to main road. **T/L**, along road for 650m going over motorway to T-junction. **T/R** & just past Jasmine Cottage on right **T/R** thro' f/g. Hg-left & thro' next f/g, hg-right followed by fc-right to just before barn. Thro' k/g on right, cross-field to go thro' f/g ahead onto road. X-stile over road on the right.

8. **H/L** cross-field thro' k/g, right of lone tree (or farm house). **Fwd** to pick up hg-right & go thro' f/g gap. **Fwd** hg-right until hedge turns right, **fwd** cross-field to x-stile & s/b. **Fwd** towards right side of farm buildings and corner of farm track. **H/R** cross-field down to stream, & go over culvert. **T/L**, stream left, to field corner.

9. **Fwd** over s/b & thro' p/g. **V/R** cross-field, aiming for left of farm buildings ahead. Thro' p/g, **T/R** & **fwd** on road to go thro' p/g (in f/g) ahead. **Fwd** cross-field to go thro' k/g ahead. **Fwd** cross field to go thro' another k/g. **Fwd** over bridle path, thro' gap, to continue hg-right. Over track to x-stile ahead. **Fwd** cross-field to cross stiles & ditch on left of lone tree ahead. **H/L** to pick up hg-left to reach field corner. X- stile and thro' hedge to continue on the same line as last field, down cross-field to reach p/gs. Thro' gates to go up cross-field keeping parallel to hedge on near right, aim for left of bungalows. X-stile **directly** onto road, pavement to right, cross into Overstone Rd, **fwd** to parking area.

Route A At the end of Note 3 **T/R** up road to enter Ansty Golf Club on right. **Fwd** drive passing clubhouse on right to go under canal bridge. **T/R**, canal embankment right for approx. 150m past bridge on right to WMP. **T/L** across course to reach & **T/L** at railway, keep as near as is practical to fence on right for 700m. Exit course via stile off corner, up walkway and x-stile onto road. **T/R** along main road, 250m after Withybrook junction x-stile on right. Continue with Note 8.

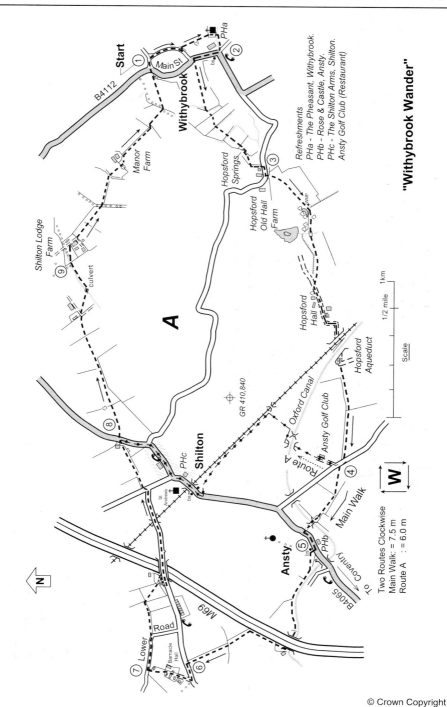

"Withybrook Wander"

Refreshments
PHa - The Pheasant, Withybrook.
PHb - Rose & Castle, Ansty.
PHc - The Shilton Arms, Shilton.
Ansty Golf Club (Restaurant)

Two Routes Clockwise
Main Walk: — = 7.5 m
Route A ··· = 6.0 m

Scale
1 km   1/2 mile

GR 410,840

↓8/12/10   B

Start : Ansty, Rose & Castle
Grid Ref. SP 399,834
Direction : Clockwise
Main Walk : = 8.0 miles
Route A : = 5.5 miles
OS Maps : (p = part)
: Landranger 140
: Pathfinder 935p
: Pathfinder 936p
: Explorer 221p
: Explorer 222p
Refreshments : (page 100
Navigation Inn, White Lion,
& Rule & Compass in or
near Bulkington.
Rose & Castle, Ansty.
Golf Club Restaurant, Ansty.
Shilton Arms, Shilton.
Pub.Transport : (page 101
Start 74 & 75.
Note There is a frequent
service No 56 to Bulkington
from Bedworth or Nuneaton.

Parking : Customers, please
ask permission to use Public
House car park.

Snippets:-
There is a new area of
woodland just to the north of
Hollyhurst Farm.

Brief information and outline of route

Starting at **Ansty** (see page 62) follow the Oxford Canal, go under the M69 and turn right up to **Barnacle** village (*Bernhangre* in DB, wooded slope by a barn). Knights Hospitallers held land at Barnacle that was a place of some note in its early days.

Then across fields to Bulkington Bridge that crosses over the Coventry Canal; the Navigation Inn sits beside it. Follow a track above the canal to go over Wem Brook then cross fields to go over the railway bridge to Weston in Arden. Past the stable block, built in 1896 to serve the nearby manor. During the Second World War it was used by the Bulkington Home Guard and later fell into disrepair. In 1988 it was restored and converted into private dwellings.

Past Weston Hall grounds, now a hotel, the Hall was originally a 16th century manor house. The three gables on the south front are Elizabethan in origin, with the extension on the left built in 1893. There is believed to have been a manor on this site dating back to 1277.

On now into **Bulkington** itself (*Bochintone* in DB, estate of a man called Bulca). George Elliot knew the village well and referred to it as Raveloe in the book of Silas Marner. Past the church of St James dating from the 13th century. The churchyard is noted for its table tombs. One standing to the right of the porch is to the memory of Mr and Mrs Johnson, uncle and aunt of George Elliot, whom she portrayed as Uncle and Aunt Pullet in The Mill on the Floss.

Now turn south past the White Lion, across the fields and under the M69, then over the railway into **Shilton** (see page 62), which once had its own station on the LMS Railway. Follow the railway for a short way and cross Ansty Golf Course and up the field into Ansty village.

Weston Hall - Bulkington

Maureen Harris

Wildlife

This area marks the transition from the Dunsmore area into the High Cross Plateau. This is a relatively flat landscape underlain by glacial deposits comprised of clays, sands, chalk and flint. Unlike the Dunsmore, this area is much less acidic and appears to have higher agricultural productivity.

The land bounded by the B4109 and the railway line to the south has a very regimented grid-like field pattern typical of a late Enclosures Act. However, outside of this area field size becomes noticeably larger with relatively few stiles to cross.

This is an area that is intensively farmed and appears to have relatively little wildlife value. However, the grassland areas to the east of Ansty are particularly rich with flood meadow species such as great burnet, meadowsweet and bird's foot-trefoil. Skylarks nest throughout much of the area and their continuous stream of high-pitched twittering song in spring is overpowering.

Barnacle Lane

A small reclamation project converted a former refuse tip and associated wetland in Bulkington into a 'natural' area. Native trees and shrubs have been planted, paths created and marshes and pond areas excavated to provide a variety of different habitats.

Maureen Harris

Gate-post to converted stable block

More Snippets :-

After Bulkington Bridge and just before the chalet style house, look back at the view towards Coventry. It is dominated by the spider web formed by the overhead pylon wires, which are terminated at the large substation near Hawkesbury Junction.

The stable block, referred to on the previous page, gained an award from The Bedworth Society "For outstanding environmental improvement 1988".

Note the plaque on the gate-post

Main Walk

1. X-stile opposite the Rose & Castle. **H/L** cross-field passing telegraph post to canal side. **Fwd** canal left, x- stile & k/g to go under motorway bridge (M69). As you exit, **fwd** thro' k/g, **T/R** up thro' k/g in hedge ahead, keep motorway right up into field corner. **T/L,** hg-right continue up to corner & x-stile just off field corner. **Fwd** hg-right, x-stile & s/b leading to road.

2. **T/L** for 130m along road, **T/R** & enter drive to Hall & immediately x-stile on left. **H/R** cross -field to x-stile with village beyond. **H/R**, hg-right to go thro' walkway between gardens. At road **T/R** & then follow hedge of house on left (No43) around to enter field. **Fwd** fc-left to x-stile & **H/L** to "outward" hedge corner. **T/R** to end of field & x-stile to road.
(**Route A** see below).

3. **T/L** up Spring Road opposite, just before cattle grid x-double stile on right. **Fwd** hg-right, at outward hedge corner, **fwd** cross-field to cross 4m footbridge ahead. Cross-field to far left corner, x-stile, **fwd** on track fc-left to corner. **T/R**, ignore gap, **T/L**, hg-left to x-fence/stile onto road.

4. **T/L** along road for 5m & **T/R** into wide shale track, **fwd** (pools on left) to reach WMP. **H/R** cross-field, aim for right of farm buildings to join & cross farm track into field. **T/L** & **V/R** cross-field over s/b, cross-field thro' young trees to far right ranch fence corner under OPL. **Fwd** to hedge, **T/L** hg-right & shortly **T/R** thro' p/g. **Fwd** hg-right, then cross-field on left using waymark directions to x-stile onto road. Opposite (WMP) enter track, next to canal. **Fwd** along track to cross f/b on right, up bank to meet fc-right. Keep fc-right for approx 50m (WMP), veer slightly left down bank and up to cross-field under OPL aiming for white building in distance to WMP in small hedge gap. **H/R** cross-field to right of pylon, **fwd** under OPL to WMP right of chalet style house. At WMP cross <u>over</u> cart track & **fwd** with house on left to reach & go over railway. **H/R** cross-field to hedgeline (WMP), **T/L**, hg-right to corner, **T/R** hg-right to road.

5. **T/L** along road to junction, cross & **T/R** down main road to where it bends right, continue **fwd** along walkway (house No 25a on left). Over road, walkway into park, cross on asphalt path to far right corner, **T/L** along road to mini-island. **T/R**, pass shops, as road bends right, **fwd** down road to Boys Club. At corner **fwd** on the left side of club enter a public space and keep on cinder path fc/trees-right. Leave path where it bends left, **fwd** over f/b in right corner to enter field, **T/L** hg-left.

6. Cross over track, hg & then fc-left for 850m to go over f/b. Cross-field, hg-right for 300m, keep on same line towards motorway, just right of a pair wooden power poles to x-stile onto track. **T/L** to steps onto main road, **T/R** under M69, **T/R** over steps to track, **fwd** 100m to x-stile on left, **fwd** 10m to x-stile on left. Cross-field to go thro' p/g, **fwd** to x-stile into small estate. **Fwd**, **T/R**, **T/L** green right, **fwd** down to main road.

7. **T/R** along road over bridge, **T/L** down concrete path and keep railway on left to exit onto main road. **T/R** and in 75m x-stile on left, down walkway to x-stile into golf course (look out for flying golf balls). **T/L** to railway fence & stay as close to fence as possible for 700m to a WMP just before bridge over railway & prominent tree. **T/R**, thro' two small birch copses, aim left of hut to WMP. **T/R**, canal bank left, ignore canal bridge to **T/L** <u>under canal</u> and pass clubhouse to road. **T/L**, shortly x-stile on right, **V/R** cross-field to hedge line, keep hg-left go thro' k/g in fence, hg-left to go thro' k/g into greenway, **fwd** over bridge, thro' p/g & up thro' hedged path to main road. **T/L** down road to Rose & Castle.

Route A

At end of Note 2 **fwd** along road to where it turns sharp left. Thro' f/g ahead, hg-right to just before railway. Over metal/fence stile go under railway. **Fwd** cross-field to go thro' large gap ahead. Now on farm track, hg-right, **fwd** up farm track until it bears right. **Fwd** cross-field to hedge do not go over f/b unless visiting Bulkington. **T/R**, hg-left to pick up Note 6.

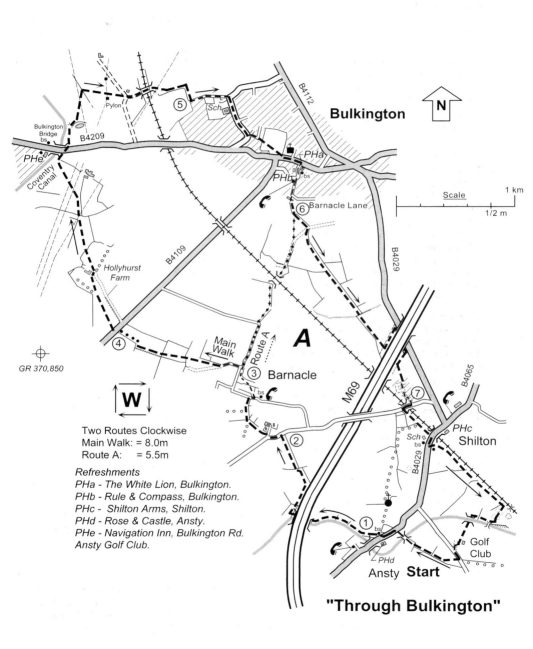

Bulkington

N

B4112

PHa

PHb
bs

⑥ Barnacle Lane

Pylon

Sch

⑤

Bulkington
Bridge
bs

B4209

PHe

Coventry
Canal

Hollyhurst
Farm

B4109

Scale

1 km

1/2 m

B4029

GR 370,850

④

Main
Walk

Route A

A

③ **Barnacle**

W

② bs

M69

⑦ **Shilton**

PHc
Sch
bs

B4029

B4065

Two Routes Clockwise
Main Walk: = 8.0m
Route A: = 5.5m

Refreshments
PHa - The White Lion, Bulkington.
PHb - Rule & Compass, Bulkington.
PHc - Shilton Arms, Shilton.
PHd - Rose & Castle, Ansty.
PHe - Navigation Inn, Bulkington Rd.
Ansty Golf Club.

① bs

PHd

Ansty **Start**

Golf
Club

"Through Bulkington"

Start : *Hawkesbury Junction*
North Coventry.
Grid Ref. SP 362,845
Direction : Clockwise
Main walk : = 8.0 miles
Route A : = 6.0 miles
OS Maps : Landranger 140
: Pathfinder 935
: Explorer 221
Refreshments : (page 100
The Greyhound,
Hawkesbury.
Rose & Crown, Ansty.
Elephant & Castle,
Aldermans Green.
Pub. Transport : (page 101
Start 30a, 30c, 37 & 60.
On or near route 74 & 75.
Parking : As you enter
Hawkesbury Junction park
in the public spaces on your
left before reaching public
house. Please ask
permission to use public
house area.

Snippets:- An extension to
this walk for a good canal
"day" is to start at the Canal
Basin in Coventry at the top of
Bishop Street. Walk out to
Hawkesbury Junction,
complete "The Canal Trail"
and return back to the Basin.
Alternatively, use public
transport back to Coventry
from Hawkesbury. Car
parking, refreshments and
toilets are all available at the
Canal Basin.
Leaflets giving more
information on the Sculpture
Trail, Old Weavers Cottages
and Courtaulds can be
obtained from Coventry
Information Centre. The
mileage for this route would
be increased by 11 miles.
Snippets contd. on next page

Brief Information and Outline of Route

This walk starts at **Hawkesbury Junction,** but if you walk back towards Coventry for a short distance the sculpture "Wings over Water" by Walenty Pytel can be seen on the bridge. The junction is formed by the Coventry and Oxford canals and is known locally as Sutton Stop. Named after the Sutton family, well known lock keepers for over half the 19th century. Richard and his son Henry are both buried in the United Reformed churchyard on Old Church Road. Since 1976 the area has been designated as a statutory Conservation Area.

By the end of 1769 the first boat loads of coal were passing through Hawkesbury between Bedworth and Coventry. The first junction between the Oxford and Coventry Canals was constructed in 1803, widened in 1836 and the connection bridged in 1837. The bridge is perhaps the most immediately striking feature in the Conservation Area. This cast iron structure is a fine example of the Victorian engineer's art, and has a span of 50 feet. The bridge was cast at the Britannia Foundry in Derby, and was erected for the Coventry Canal Company in 1837 at a cost of £630. The abutments are made of red hand-made bricks with a semicircular blue brick coping. This style of bridge, and combination of materials, was adopted between 1800-1840 on some of the Midland canals. Their use in this bridge shows a lightness of design unexpected with such heavy materials.

By 1830 the Engine House and Toll Offices and, what is now the Greyhound Inn, were all in use. After the Second World War the commercial traffic declined and the feature of the last few years has been the greatly increased interest in canals and canal cruising in particular.

The engine or pump house is perhaps the most unusual and interesting of all the buildings in the Conservation Area, both historically and architecturally. The lean-to at the rear is the oldest part and housed the first engine to be installed in 1821. This was a Newcomen type engine which had already seen around one hundred years service at one of the local collieries. It was named "Lady Godiva" and used to raise water into the canal from a stream flowing underneath. By 1837, however, this supply proved inadequate, a 114 foot shaft was sunk and a new, more powerful engine installed alongside "Lady Godiva" in the handsome three-storey building which now fronts the canal. In 1913 this water supply failed due to the sinking of the new Coventry Colliery and the engine house fell into disuse. The newer engine was scrapped during the Second World War. "Lady Godiva" remained in place until 1963 when it was moved to Dartmouth, the birthplace of Thomas Newcomen, as the centrepiece of a memorial museum.

Waterway Network: Oxford Canal: History

1769 The first Act of Parliament allowing the construction of the Oxford Canal was passed. James Brindley was originally the engineer on the project but he died in 1772.

1790 The canal was opened. It was one of the earliest contour built canals, engineered by Brindley. The day the canal was opened into Oxford the price of coal fell by 50%.

1830 Improvement works resulted in the northern section of the canal being shortened by 14 miles.

Turn right at **Bedworth Hill Bridge** and cross the fields to Barnacle. Through **Barnacle** (see page 66), cross the fields under the M69 to join the Oxford Canal at Ansty (see page 62). Cross over the canal at the rear of the Rose and Castle and join the towpath to go west meeting the noisy M6 on the left and Sowe Common on the right. Keep along the canal passing a fishing tackle shop and the Elephant and Castle on the left and then back through a conglomeration of power station bits and pieces to **Hawkesbury**.

Wildlife

The presence of a variety of fresh water mussel species that live in the Oxford Canal is a testament to the high quality water in this waterway. To the casual observer the canal appears to be of poor habitat quality with little adjacent habitat either side. However, the canal contains a strong population of water vole and even supports an extensive population of the increasingly rare white clawed (or Atlantic) crayfish (which looks a bit like a small lobster). This species has suffered tremendous population losses due to the introduction of the much larger American signal crayfish.

The larger size of the signal crayfish, favoured in preference to the much smaller native breed by fish farmers, impacts upon the breeding success of white clawed crayfish. However, the real problem has been a fungal disease carried by the signal crayfish that our native species has no resistance to. This has resulted in entire river populations of white clawed crayfish being wiped out. Pollution and river engineering hasn't helped remaining populations of white clawed crayfish, which are now legally protected from capture and selling.

Snippets continued:-
This walk starts at the same place as The Sowe Valley Footpath, a 8.5 mile walk through a ribbon park. Although mainly urban across Coventry (north-south) it has plenty of interest and wildlife. A coloured leaflet can be obtained from the City Development Directorate, see page 104.
The walk can be used to shorten the 40 mile "A Coventry Way" by using the Footpath to connect Walks 15 to 5 or vice versa.
Canal trips are available, enquire at Coventry Canal Basin.

Possibly the most diverse area in terms of habitats occurs within and around the area known as Hawkesbury Junction. The interaction between the urban fringe, past industrial land and the countryside has resulted in a mix of agricultural land, recreational land and areas of overgrown wilderness. The presence of the canal and a complex of wetland and open water features add to the diversity of this area, which is rich in bird life. The lucky (or observant) may be rewarded on warm, sunny days by seeing grass snakes.

Grass Snake

Main Walk

1. From The Greyhound go over the large arched bridge, go left of building ahead (WMP "Your Green Track"), **fwd** under f/b. **Fwd** canal left to the first bridge over the canal (Bedworth Hill Bridge, do not go under or over).

2. Before bridge exit up to track. **T/R** & follow main track. After first OPL x-stile on left. **V/R**, thro' young trees to k/g. **Fwd** (pool right) thro' another k/g. **T/R** then **T/L**, hg-right, bank left to outward hedge corner. **Fwd** on track, pass pool on right then thro' gap by gate and ahead onto road.

3. **T/L** for 5m, x-stile on right. **Fwd** hg-right to outward corner, **T/R** and then after gap **T/L**, f/c-right to x-stile. **V/L** to cross-field and go over f/b. **Fwd** cross-field to pick up hg-left at outward hedge corner, x-stiles into road. **T/L (fwd)** down road to junction.

4. On opposite side of road x-stile on right, **V/L** to pick up hg-left to outward hedge corner, **H/L** to x-stile in right hand fence and **fwd** fc-right to green. **T/R** at road and shortly **T/L** at WMP along walkway between houses. Enter field, hg-left to WMP, approx. 75m before field corner ahead. **(Route A** see below).

5. Continue **fwd** hg-left to its end, **fwd** cross-field to x-stile into drive close to road. **T/R** to road, **T/L** for 130m to go over s/b on right & x-stile.

6. Hg-left to field corner, x-stile and pick up hg-left down to M69 boundary. **T/R**, M69 left to go thro' k/g down to canal thro' k/g on left, **fwd** under M69, thro' k/g and with canal right x-stile. **H/L** cross-field away from canal aiming up left of white pub to x-stile onto road.

7. Over road to Rose and Castle & walk down to the canal thro' car park. Over bridge **T/R**, canal right, under M69 to third bridge over canal (No 9) (Sowe Common & junction with Route A).

8. Continue **fwd**, canal right until you get to Hawkesbury Junction.

Cast Iron Bridge at Hawkesbury

Engine or Pump House at Hawkesbury

Route A.

At the end of Note 4, **T/R** at WMP to cross-field, parallel to hedge on left to go thro' large gap at field boundary. **Fwd** hg-right until next gap, <u>do not go through</u>. Keeping in same field, **H/L**, hg-right to go thro' gap in field corner. Hg-right to cross waymarked fence in field corner. Hg-right, to pass small copse on right, **T/L** & shortly **T/R**, hg-right to go thro' small gap in field corner. Hg-right to x-stile into allotment area. **Fwd**, hg-right, under OPL thro' k/g to walkway onto road. **T/L** to junction with main road. Cross over, **T/R**, & shortly **V/L** into Woodway Lane, **fwd** across Sowe Common to go over canal bridge. **T/R** at end of bridge to pick up tow path and main route at Note 8.

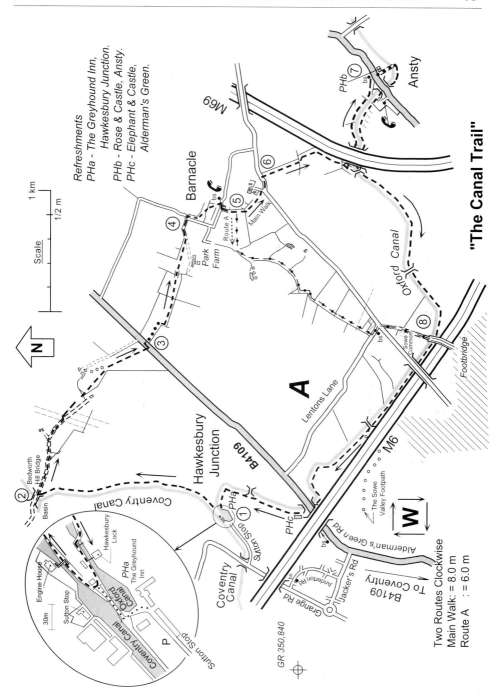

Refreshments
PHa - The Greyhound Inn,
Hawkesbury Junction.
PHb - Rose & Castle, Ansty.
PHc - Elephant & Castle,
Alderman's Green.

Scale
1/2 m
1 km

Barnacle

Ansty

M69

Oxford Canal

Park Farm

Route A
Main Walk

Hawkesbury Junction

B4109

Lentons Lane

M6

Sowe Common

Footbridge

The Sowe Valley Footpath

Coventry Canal

Bedworth Hill Bridge
Basin

Hawkesbury Lock

Engine House

Sutton Stop

Oxford Canal

Coventry Canal

PHa The Greyhound Inn

30m

P

Sutton Stop

Coventry Canal

PHc

PHb

GR 350,840

Alderman's Green Rd

Grange Rd
Anderton Rd
Jacker's Rd

B4109
To Coventry

"The Canal Trail"

Two Routes Clockwise
Main Walk: = 8.0 m
Route A   : = 6.0 m

© Crown Copyright

Start : Corley Ash
Junction of Tamworth Rd &
Square Lane.
Grid Ref. SP 294,861
Direction : Clockwise
Main Walk: = 7.5 miles
Route A   : = 6.0 miles
OS Maps : Landranger 140
**   : Pathfinder 935**
**   : Explorer   221**
Refreshments : ℓ page 100
Saracen's Head, Corley Ash.
Royal Oak, South Bedworth.
Golden Eagle, Keresley
Village.
Horse & Jockey, Corley.
Fish and Chips, Bennett's
Road North, Keresley End.
Pub. Transport : ℓ page 101
Start 735.
On or near route 56 &57.
also West Midlands No 36.
Parking : Carefully in lay-by
near Saracen's Head or as a
customer in public house
car park.

Brief information and outline of route

This walk starts at The Saracen's Head, **Corley Ash**. Cross Tamworth Road to go off Square Lane and back down to the modern fishing pool in the area known as Savage's Square. Turn left and walk up more of Square Lane, crossing Breach Brook.

Cross fields on right. On the left in these fields can be seen the remains of an ack-ack site . The Royal Artillery army camp consisted of approximately 14 huts and a radar cabin. These were manned by 110 gunners and auxiliary staff. The site was established just after the November blitz on Coventry in 1940.

Continue on Breach Oak Lane and over the stile towards Breach Oak Farm and on across relatively remote country to Vaul's Farm. Then cross more fields to Astley Lane and down beside Astley Hall Farm to Goodyears End, on the outskirts of **Bedworth**.

Over the M6 cross Breach Brook again past Newland Hall Farm and the Golden Eagle to **Keresley** (*Keresleia* in 1144, possibly a woodland clearing of a man called Cenhere). Keresley Green was a significant mining village up until the late twentieth century.

Across the fields and turn right at Hall Yard Wood and along to the lane past Burrow Hill, an Iron Age Fort (and now an Ancient Monument) to **Corley** (*Cornelie* in DB, a clearing frequented by herons or cranes).

Past Corley Rocks, a sandstone outcrop on the right, an attraction for Coventry youngsters over many years. Between the wars a cycle out to the rocks from Coventry was quite an adventure, revived by a bottle of cold tea and a race back home.

Carry on down Rock Lane and turn left before Bob's Wood. Further down the lane past the wood is Corley Hall, immortalised in George Elliot's Adam Bede, it appears as Hall Farm. It is believed to have been built in the 16th century. Back up the lane and over fields towards and then under the M6 to **Corley Ash**.

Wildlife

An area typical of the Ancient Arden landscape, containing frequent medium-sized woodland blocks, connected by a myriad of meandering hedgerows with associated ditches and small streams. This provides an interesting contrast to the relatively woodless landscape to the east of Bedworth, with its straight-hedged rectangular field pattern.

Many of the woodlands are dominated by oak and hazel, with a ground flora of bluebell. However, in many cases oak has been replaced by sycamore, which became a popular timber wood in the 19th century, with uses such as cabinet veneers and violins. The connecting hedgerows

Snippets:- *Breach Brook is a tributary of the River Sowe, (M6/A444). The walk crosses it twice as it follows the relatively high ground around this watercourse.*

This green logo is seen all the way round A Coventry Way.

It is either a small sticker or a 75mm (3in) disk.
The 40 mile Long Distance Path is designated on the Ordnance Survey Explorer series 221 and 222 and on the latest Landranger 140.

are often ancient and contain a wide variety of woody species, which often include a woodland ground flora. Look out for bluebell and wood anemone early in the year.

The area is noted for its high density of farm ponds, associated with land used for cattle rearing. Such clusters of farm ponds are increasingly rare and it is suggested that over the last 50 years about 50% of the ponds in Britain have been lost. Over 50% of the remaining ponds have become heavily shaded and are partially silted up or have been stocked with fish. Great crested newts will likely occur in many of the ponds in this area and, in some cases, a local population will have established itself within a cluster of ponds. Great crested newts are protected through national and international legislation. Britain holds approximately 90% of the global population of this species and estimates of up to 75% loss of suitable pond habitat is a major concern. A recent local survey of ponds, which included this area, has revealed that about 25% of ponds still contain great crested newts, although a high proportion are in a poor condition.

Ancient Times

O ne of our members wrote this short article for A Coventry Way Association Newsletter in 2001:
The paths which form "A Coventry Way" in the Corley area may well have been trodden for hundreds of years and there is evidence of human activity going back thousands of years. Visible evidence is the site of an Iron Age Fort above Corley Rocks that goes back some two-and-a-half thousand years. Last summer in a garden along Breach Oak Lane to the north of Corley Rocks, very close to the point where "A Coventry Way" meets the lane (GR 308,871), I came across a small piece of flint at less than a spades depth. Flint is not native to the area. It was the size of a fifty pence coin, flattish, roughly

Typical Flint Tool

triangular with rounded corners. As I cleaned the object I could see that two sides had been chipped and formed straight sharp edges. Warwick Museum identified it as a Stone Age tool, that could be used for small tasks, cutting meat and scraping animal skins, typical of the new Stone Age 4000 - 2300 years B.C. The flint originated from a site near Hinckley. In the last forty years a dense scatter of hundreds of various Stone Age flint objects have been found in fields to the south of Corley Rocks. It could indicate it has been a settlement, or a place of concentrated work. A Romano-British bronze knife handle and medieval pottery have also been found. Plodding across ploughed fields may seem boring, but you never know what items from the past you may be lucky enough to find.

A 1918 Poster - supplied by Mike Murray

Main Walk

1. From the junction walk down Square Lane for 80m & go thro' f/g on left. **Fwd** cross-field thro' p/g ahead, **fwd** hg-right to corner. **T/R,** thro' gap hg-left round to left & WMP. **T/R** cross-field down to outer corner of conifer hedge. X-stile into fishing pool area, **T/R** pool left to x-stile onto road. **T/L** up road for 400m over s/b and thro' k/g on right.

2. **Fwd** hg-left to go thro p/g (in f/g) on left, **T/R**, hg-right to its end, continue **fwd** to **T/L** thro' paddocks via k/gs, **fwd** thro' k/g onto road (100m before farm). **T/R** along road to junction. **Fwd** for 20m to x-stile on left adjacent to gate into farm drive.

3. Up drive to go thro' p/g (in f/g) on right. **T/L, T/R** round corner hg-left to shortly x-stile on left into paddock. **Fwd** bank/fc/hg-left and at outward corner **H/L** to x-stile into large field. **Fwd** hg-left for approx. 800m, ignoring wide hedge gap on left, continue   hg-left. **T/L** thro' k/g on left into farm area. **T/R** away from buildings down to p/g in fence ahead. **(Route A** see below).

4. Thro' p/g, **fwd** cross-field down to WMP , junction of streams at far corner. Cross over culvert, left of junction. **T/R,** stream right, to cross culvert, **fwd** stream right on right. **T/L,** hg-right to x-stile & thro' k/g shortly on right. Spinney left & then hg-left thro' f/g to x-stile to road. **T/R** up **busy** road over stream for 250m to x-stile on right (20m past the fourth pole on right).

5. Up bank, fence right to outward corner, **fwd** to x-stile opposite & s/b to road. Cross over road & **fwd** down Whitburn Rd, as road turns left **fwd** into walkway right side of house. **Fwd** over road into walkway & then playing field. Hg-right under OPL to corner, **fwd** cross-field to meet hedge, short right and **T/L** to cross-field, thro' k/g to main road. **T/L** down road to junction & keep right over M6.

6. Shortly thro' k/g on right along walkway into field, go **left,** hg-left down to go over f/b (Breach Brook), x-stile, **T/R** to stile, **T/L in front** of stile & up 200m to meet hg corner, hg-right under OPL. X-stile, hg-right, short field, farm buildings on left to x-2 stiles. Continue

hg-right until field narrows, look for stile in left hand hedge. Cross stile and **T/R** into sports field. Hg-right along bank to enter walkway at right hand end of concrete fence before Golden Eagle. **Fwd** along back of houses to main road. **T/R** along road, over Grove Lane, **fwd** on pavement for another 100m to cross road to WMP **on left,** enter drive to houses.

7. At end of drive left of house enter walkway, hg-left, fence panels right. **Fwd** up enclosed "copse area" to x-stile, up left into field, **T/R** hg-right to top corner. Thro' f/g gap on right, **T/L** hg-left to go thro' f/g gap on left at end of field. **T/R** to pick up hg-right & continue up hill to the top. Keep hg-right as it comes down to field corner & thro' k/g. **T/R** at waymark post, hg-right up small valley, over large hedge gap, hg-right to go thro' k/g off field corner onto road. **T/R** down road, pass Corley Rocks on right, continue down to junction right. Over junction down road for 200m to go thro' k/g on left. (This field has a wood starting on its right boundary.)

8. Up field hg-left to outward corner, **V/R** to top hedge line & x-stile near corner with wire fence. Hg-right passing knoll on left to x-stile. Pick up hg-right for approx. 60m to x-stile on right into next field. **H/L** to go under OPL & go over stile next to f/g. **V/R** to aim for bottom (left) field corner next to M6. **T/L,** motorway right, x-stile then over 2 fields to main road. **T/R** under motorway to finish.

Route A At the end of Note 3: **T/R** at fence to go thro' k/g, **fwd** to pick up hg-right. Thro' f/g over culvert, **fwd** hg-left to x-stile. Hg-left to x-stile next to gate. **Fwd** along lane to main road, **T/R & T/L** to go thro' f/g on left, **fwd** hg-left to x-stile hg-left round pool on left down to enter copse in corner via a f/b. Up bank with steps & x-stile continue **fwd** with waymark arrow to meet M6 boundary. **T/L,** M6 right, x-stile to exit copse, **fwd** M6 right. X-stile **fwd** up & **T/R** over M6 & down right to x-stile into field, **fwd** to x-stile in corner of left hedge. Hedge near right up to x-double stile, under OPL & continue hg-right to x-stile into walkway. Along walkway to main road. Cross straight over, enter drive & continue with Note 7.

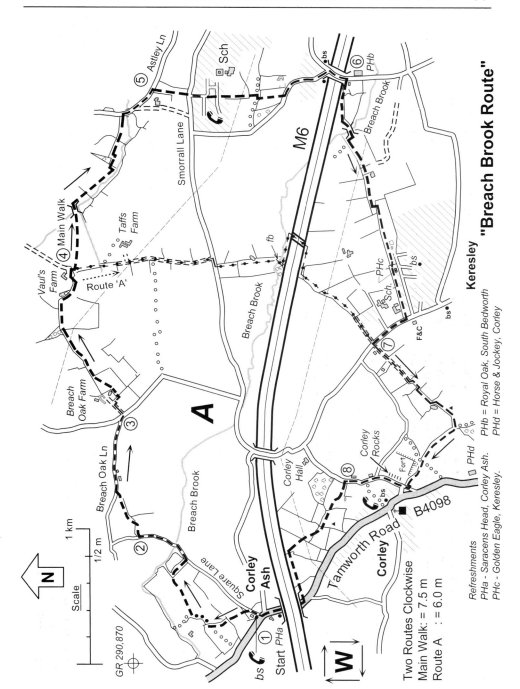

"Breach Brook Route"

Keresley

Refreshments
PHa - Saracens Head, Corley Ash.
PHc - Golden Eagle, Keresley.
PHb = Royal Oak, South Bedworth
PHd = Horse & Jockey, Corley

Two Routes Clockwise
Main Walk: = 7.5 m
Route A   : = 6.0 m

GR 290, 870

Scale

N

1 km

1/2 m

© Crown Copyright

10/4/20

Start : Fillongley, junction of Coventry Rd & Church Lane
Grid Ref. SP 281,871
Direction : Clockwise
Main Walk: = 5.5 miles
Route A   : = 4.0 miles
For extended route see page 79
OS Maps : Landranger 140
**   : Pathfinder 935**
**   : Explorer   221**
Refreshments : ℓ page 100
Manor House, Fillongley.
Butchers Arms, Fillongley.
Weavers Arms, Fillongley.
Saracen's Head, Corley Ash.
Pub. Transport : ℓ page 101
Start 735.
Parking : Carefully in Church Lane.

Snippets:-
The Ring and Bailey at the end of this walk has remained a mystery as we cannot find anything about it.
There is also some talk of a third castle where artifacts have been found.
One of the locals described one ROW as being established due to it being the mole catcher's route to work!
The bridge, refurbished by a nearby resident, that you go over to enter back into Fillongley village is called Pegasus Bridge by some locals to commemorate a nearby resident's experience in the Second World War.

Brief Information and Outline of Route

This walk starts in **Fillongley** (*Filingelei* in DB, woodland clearing of the family of followers of Fygla). In this elevated village are two earthworks, one bearing the name of Castle Hills and the other Castle Yard (Ring and Bailey on map). Walk down Church Lane past the 14th century church of St Mary & All Saints with many artifacts from a forgotten time, like an immensely tall cross in the grounds which must have been there for over 500 years. There is also a wooden cross made from fragments of wood picked up in the remnants of a shattered Belgian church during the First World War.

On past the old Methodist church, now a private house. Over the main road, up Berryfields past Priest Cottages. These seven cottages were built in 1893 at the same time as the Methodist chapel. They were homes for retired preachers. Up and past Berryfields Farm, as you climb up the hill glimpse back to see the Motte and Bailey on "Castle Hills". (On route A the site is on the right over the stream

The Cross at St Mary and All Saints

Kevin Wilkins

and is on private land.) This is a small, well preserved entrenchment. Oval in shape covering approximately one acre, it's reputed to be of Saxon origin. All that remains are the earthworks and an outer ditch and banked enclosure. The ditch or moat was probably once filled with water from a stream that still runs on the south-west side.

Up to Tipper's Hill Farm with its good views and turn south-east to Wood End. Towards the Weaver's Arms, not so surprisingly called because a family of weavers once lived there, then head south passing through the gardens of Big House Farm down to Square Lane. Pass through the fishing pool area at Savage's Square, up to skirt Red Hill Farm and through a private garden onto the Coventry

Road. Over the fields south west then north to the later earthworks on the site known as Castle Yard (Ring and Bailey on OS maps). It lies on a triangle of land formed by the junction of two brooks. At the apex of this triangle rises a low mount or keep; south of this is a courtyard, which occupies an area of over an acre, lying between the brooks. A moat surrounds the mound and the court, through the eastern side of which one of the streams runs, while water sometimes stands within it on the west. There are remnants of a rampart running round inside the moat upon the south side of the court. On the summit of the mount there are remains of masonry. Continue the walk past Castle Farm down to Coventry Road to reach The Manor.

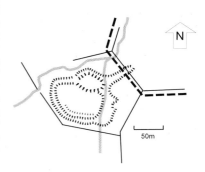

Route through Ring and Bailey at Castle Yard, Fillongley

Wood Anemone

Wildlife

A pleasant summer walk with small patches of grassland, road verges and hedges to explore. Perhaps the most interesting location in terms of wildlife habitats is the Ring and Bailey which includes dry grassland banks, wet hollows and woodland scrub. Mouse-ear hawkweed, field woodrush, pignut, yarrow, cat's ear, bird's foot trefoil and bulbous buttercup occur on the drier grasslands. The wet hollows contain numerous rush species with lady's smock, lesser celandine and nettles. Also includes ash woodland with abundant hawthorn, alder, holly and crab apple with bluebell, dog's mercury, foxglove and wood anemone.

Extended Route

Once on top of Tipper's Hill you can, if you wish, have a look at the views to the north by extending this route.

During Note 2 "instead of **T/R** between two pools along green lane". **Fwd** with hg-right to x-stile in corner. **T/R** down farm track to road. **T/R** up road, just past cottage on left climb up steps in steep bank <u>on right</u> to x-stile. **V/R** cross-field to x-stile into green lane. **T/R** and shortly x-stile on left, pick up route in Note 2 at "initially **fwd**".

Main Walk

1. **Fwd** along Church Lane to reach the Nuneaton Road (B4102). **Fwd** over to go along opposite road (Berry Fields), left at junction, down thro' 2 f/g's, **T/R** & thro' p/g (in f/g) to enter field. (**Route A** see below).

2. **Fwd,** on track thro' p/g (in f/g) then **V/L** cross-field up to top left hand corner, thro' p/g, **fwd** up cross-field under OPL to field boundary in front of farm buildings. Thro' small gap, **fwd** hg-right to x-stile, thro' walkway to x-stile into field. Hg-right to field corner (over gap), **T/L** for a short distance & **T/R** between two pools along green lane. After 15m thro' k/g on <u>right</u>, initially **fwd** cross-field to pick up hg-right to corner. Thro' k/g, **H/L** plus cross-field <u>parallel to OPL</u> on right to go thro' f/g in corner. **Fwd** cross-field under pylon to go thro' k/g, **fwd** cross-field leaving hedge on right to go thro' k/g ahead onto road.

3. **T/R** & cross road (**with care**), just before The Weavers Arms x-stile on left. **V/L** cross-field to outward corner (laurel hedge) to go thro k/g in corner, along walkway to road. **T/R** along road (pavement), passing cottages on right to x-stile on left opposite Wood End House. Hg-right for 200m, over s/b on right thro' p/g, **T/L**, hg-left (ditch) to corner. **T/R** at tree stump, hg-left for 180m to go thro' p/g & over s/b on left, **T/R**, hg-right up to go thro' p/g into garden, thro' second p/g, hg-right to join house drive near & onto road.

4. **T/L** & immediately **T/R** down road. **Fwd** down road (joining ACW) for approx. 700m to fishing pool on right, x-stile into pool area, hg/fc-left to corner of enclosure to x-stile into field. **Fwd** <u>up</u> cross-field aiming for high hedge area & WMP ahead. **T/L** hg-right.

5. Continue round to field corner, thro' gap into copse area ahead. **H/L** thro' copse on zig-zag path to WMP, **fwd** cross-field aiming for left end of conifers. Thro' p/g into garden, fc-right thro' p/g's & gate onto road. **T/R** up road to to next road junction (Wood End Lane).

6. Opposite junction thro' k/g into field. Hg-right to outer corner, **V/L** to go over s/b & thro' k/g, pass pond on left hg-left, to field corner, thro' kg, hg-left to field corner thro' k/g & over s/b. Hg-left to go over culvert thro' gap, **fwd** to pick up fence on right. Just past metal f/g x-stile on right (leaving ACW).

7. **Fwd** cross short gap to reach start of hedge, hg-left to go over f/b. Up hg-right, pass pond on right, **fwd** cross-field to go over s/b & stile. **Fwd** cross-field (short) to go thro' gap. Hg-right uphill to go thro' gap & downhill hg-right to field corner. Follow round to left (ignore gaps) & in 180m over f/b & thro' p/g on right into site of castle. Fc-right, over f/b & thro' k/g into field. **T/R**, fence & stream right for 130m, thro' p/g on right & over f/b, up steps & x-stile on left to exit into an area between houses onto road. **T/L** down road, **T/R** into Church Lane.

Route A At the end of Note 1 **T/R**, hg-right (N W Circular Walk). Fwd to corner **T/L**, then **fwd** with hg-right to go thro' p/g. Hg-right to go thro' k/g, hg-right for 40m to cross stream over f/b on right. **T/L** hg-left for 140m, **H/R** cross-field to reach metalled track at field corner. **T/R** up lane to main road & cross over to the nearby Weaver's Arms. In car park x-stile in back hedge, **H/R** cross-field to corner. X-stile, pass pond right to x-stile into field. **T/R**, hg-right, follow round to reach & go thro' p/g in garden fence. Thro' garden onto road (Sandy Lane). Thro' k/g opposite, hg-right to corner, thro' k/g on right. Hg-right for 30m, **T/L** to go thro' k/g, cross stream into field. **Fwd**, hg-right, go thro' k/g in corner. **V/R** to go thro' k/g onto road (Wood End Lane). Thro' k/g opposite into field, **V/R** cross-field downhill to field corner & thro' k/g and over s/b. **Fwd** up to incoming hg-right (WMP). Continue up & round hg-right until a WMP is reached. Continue with Note 5.

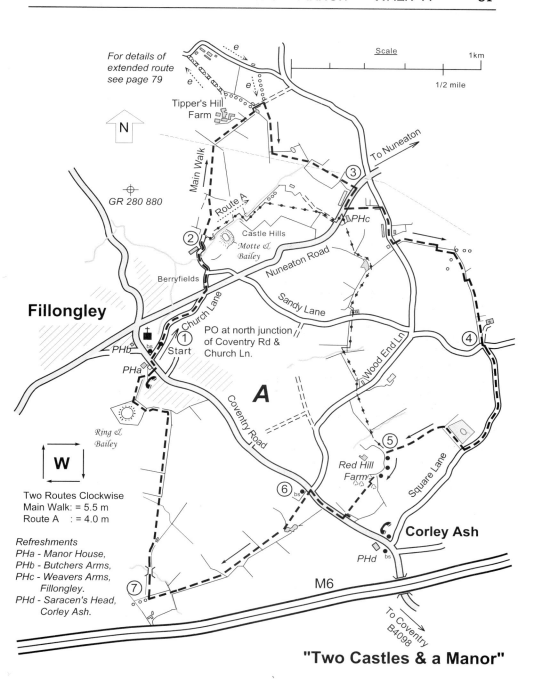

For details of
extended route
see page 79

Tipper's Hill
Farm

Scale

1km

1/2 mile

To Nuneaton

③

N

Main Walk

GR 280 880

Route A

Castle Hills

② Motte & Bailey

PHc

Berryfields

Fillongley

Church Lane

Nuneaton Road

Sandy Lane

PHb

① Start

PO at north junction
of Coventry Rd &
Church Ln.

Wood End Ln

④

PHa

A

Coventry Road

Ring & Bailey

W

Two Routes Clockwise
Main Walk: = 5.5 m
Route A   : = 4.0 m

Refreshments
PHa - Manor House,
PHb - Butchers Arms,
PHc - Weavers Arms,
        Fillongley.
PHd - Saracen's Head,
        Corley Ash.

⑤

Red Hill
Farm

Square Lane

⑥

Corley Ash

PHd

M6

⑦

To Coventry
B4098

"Two Castles & a Manor"

© Crown Copyright

Start : Corley Moor
Grid Ref. SP 279,850
Direction : Clockwise
Main Walk: = 7.5 miles
Route A : = 6.5 miles
OS Maps : Landranger 140
: Pathfinder 935
: Explorer 221
Refreshments : ℓ page 100
Bull & Butcher, Corley Moor
The Red Lion, Corley Moor
Saracen's Head, Corley Ash
Pub.Transport : ℓ page 101
Start 735.
On or near route
West Midlands 36 to
Keresley Village.
Parking : Triangle opposite
Bull and Butcher.

Snippets:- In a survey of the
area in 1411, and again in
1650, a windmill is noted as
being in the Wyndemulnefeld.

"Now the lane opens: sudden
on the right
Rich-sanded Corley Rocks
come into sight,
Red Indian paradise for feet to
scramble
Through lacing palisades of
fern and bramble"
From Corley 1901, collected
poems and epigrams of George
Rostrevor Hamilton.

The Bull and Butcher at
Corley Moor incorporated a
butcher's shop in the 1890s.
The Tin Tabernacle has been
in the past the subject of a
planning application. If
approved, it would have been
removed. It is still there in
2002. Above the porch was a
wooden spire with a single
bell. Apparently christenings,
but not marriages, were held
here until recently.

Brief Information and Outline of Route

Start at the triangle opposite the Bull & Butcher at Corley Moor. Go towards the Red Lion and turn right, pass the Rest Cottage to go across Corley Moor.

Over the M6 and across fields to Tamworth Road. Tamworth Road, dating back to the 14th century, runs along the ridge and was originally an ancient carriage way leading from Lichfield to Warwick. Turn right to go through a garden on left, cross fields to private fishing pool area at Savage's Square.

Left up Square Lane, cross fields on right (see page 74 re "ack-ack" site). Turn right along Breach Oak Lane and turn right past Astley Lodge Farm. Over Breach Brook and onto Highfield Lane, left and then right over the M6 again and past Corley Service Area.

Along Bennett's Road, turn right over fields to an outcrop of Red Sandstone to what is almost the highest point (560ft above sea level) in the area. Here stands Burrow Hill, the site of an Iron Age Fort excavated in 1926. Right at the top of Rock Lane to Corley, (Cornelie in DB, clearing frequented by cranes or herons) walk through the churchyard. The parish church was runner up (September 2001) in the best kept churchyard section of Warwickshire's best kept village competition.

Left at Church Lane and left again down to Marslands Farm, (possibly the Maisterlonde of 1403) and skirt round Little Lady Wood bearing round right to cross fields to Wall Hill Road.

Turn left past Slashpitts Farm and across the fields to come out to Watery Lane near the Mission Church (The Tin Tabernacle). Right and then left to Windmill Lane past the old windmill now a private residence, right along Wall Hill Road back to the triangle.

The Tin Tabernacle

Kevin Wilkins

Wildlife

Although a walk that can be enjoyed all year round the Three Corleys is particularly pleasant in the later part of the summer and especially during August.

On leaving the Bull and Butcher you will encounter an aspen woodland which contain some scattered oak and ash. The Latin for aspen is *Populous tremula* and this describes the shimmering effect the roundish, stiff leaves of the tree produce in a light breeze. Lords and ladies (or cuckoo pint) occur in the wood and are particularly noticeable during the late autumn when the plant's poisonous berries turn bright red.

You may wish to take a moment to consider the area of common opposite the wood. This grassland is particularly noted for its population of sneezewort and heath bedstraw, which were once common in the Coventry area. Knapweed is also present and with the rush dominated areas the wetland loving lesser stitchwort can be found.

Once over the motorway you'll encounter a pond with a good deal of emergent vegetation such as branched bur-reed, good for damselflies and dragonflies in the late summer.

Following down from Astley Lodge Farm you encounter a small copse with a shaded pool. The margins of this woodland contain foxglove which steal the show when in full bloom. To the south of the pool you'll cross Breach Brook, a canalised watercourse, which at first glance looks to be of little wildlife interest. Fool's watercress occurs in abundance, whose name suggests that it is easily confused with the edible watercress (although it is more closely related to hogweed). If lucky you may also see the small, deep blue flowers of brooklime which supports the impressive Latin title of *Veronica beccabunga*. It is worth approaching the brook as quietly as you can as it is home to the now rare water vole which, if you are very fortunate, can be seen grazing on the aquatic vegetation. Ratty has been the subject of considerable concern after its population crash in the 1970s and 80s, which has been largely due to predation by mink.

Having passed through Corley itself you may wish to linger along the edge of Little Lady Wood, a birch woodland with occasional oak and ash and an abundance of holly. Hazel, rowan and other fruiting shrubs also occur and these provide an autumnal feast for birds and woodland mammals. However, during the spring the show of bluebell provides a deep luxuriate hue into the depths of the wood.

On the final section of the walk you may wish to rest a while and take in the pleasant surrounds of Green Lane. Here you'll find bush vetch and meadow vetchling in abundance alongside lofty stands of hogweed. The blaze of colour attracts many insects, including butterflies, which can be seen feeding on warm still days.

Kevin Wilkins

Corley Moor - Lane Junction
A God Cake? One of many in this area, see page 101.

Main Walk

1. From the triangle, with your back to The Bull & Butcher go right down Wall Hill Road. **T/R** down next road. **Fwd**, down towards and onto moor before cottage on your left (ignore path going right). **Fwd** over moor to enter path thro' copse with garden boundary on your right. Thro' k/g & up steps to concrete road, **T/R** over M6 Bridge, on exiting bridge go down steps on right, thro' k/g. **H/R** cross-field to shortly go thro' another k/g. **Fwd** to pick up stile in fence, **fwd** to go over culverted stream. **Fwd** to go over hg-right and continue over three fields via k/gs. Thro' k/g near pool. **H/L** to outward field corner, hg-left to go thro' k/g onto road.

2. **T/R** down road on pavement opposite until The Laurels is reached just before Corley Village sign. Walk thro' double gates and go thro' p/gs, thro' garden fc-left, to exit into field thro' p/g. **Fwd** cross-field to zig-zag thro' copse to corner. Thro' gap hg-left round to left & WMP, **T/R** cross-field down to left hand end of hedge. X-stile into fishing pool area, **T/R** pool left to x-stile onto road. (**Route A** see below).

3. **T/L** up road for 400m, over s/b and thro' k/g on right. **Fwd** hg-left to go thro' p/g (in f/g) on left. **T/R** hg-right to its end, continue **fwd** to **T/L** thro' paddocks via k/g's, fwd thro' k/g onto road (100m before farm). **T/R** along road to a high metal clad gate on right just before road junction.

4. Thro' gate (chain loose!), follow laurel hg-right to corner, x-stile, **V/R** cross-field to x-stile left of copse. **V/L** cross-field over a f/b in hedge at bottom of field, **H/L** over culvert, **V/L** to outer field corner. X-stile, up bank to x-stile, hg-right to cross a pair of stiles adjacent to water tub. **V/R** cross-field to x-stile, up embankment onto road. **T/L** along road to junction.

5. **T/R** & pass over motorway, follow road around (pavement left) to pass service road junction on left and junction with Rock Lane on right. **Fwd** from this junction for 250m to x-stile by f/g on right. Hg-right to reach enclosed path. **Fwd** to reach track then up track, x-stile onto road. **T/R** for 50m and then **T/L**, passing Corley Rocks on left continue up road to take right junction to main road. Continue over and walk thro' the churchyard opposite to exit into Church Lane. **T/L** up road (pavement right) towards mast.

6. **T/L** just before Brownhill Cottage, thro' k/g and follow enclosed footpath, thro' k/g into field. Hg-right, bear round right to x-stile in holly hedge. Hg/fc-left almost to drive to x-stile on left, **H/R** cross-field corner to farm drive. Note that you have left the Right of Way for a "permissive" path. **Fwd** down drive and as drive bends left, go thro' f/g. **T/R**, hg-right to reach boundary of wood ahead. **T/R** and follow wood and then hedge boundary left over 2 fields via k/g's. In third field ignore k/g on left & continue hg-left up hill over another three fields to reach road.

7. **T/R** and shortly take left fork to Corley Moor. **Fwd** for approx. 250m along road, thro' second k/g on left (just past Slashpitts Farm), **H/R**, cross-field to go over stream & thro' k/g. **Fwd** cross-2-fields thro' k/gs. Enter enclosed path & go thro' 2 k/gs & x-stile onto road. **T/R** and shortly **T/L** along Green Lane, **T/R** down Windmill Lane to The Red Lion. **T/R** up road to return to triangle.

Route A

At the end of Note 2, **T/L** up road for 120m (Telegraph Pole No 17). X-stile on right, thro' p/g into enclosed path to x-stile. **V/R** cross-field to meet hedge on right. Hg-right for a short distance to x-stile & f/b on right. **Fwd** to pick up hg-right and cross two stiles with f/b in between near field corner. **H/L**, cross-field to go thro' f/g (muddy), **fwd** on same line to x-stile near corner of field before farm house. **T/L** along road to junction to continue with Note 5.

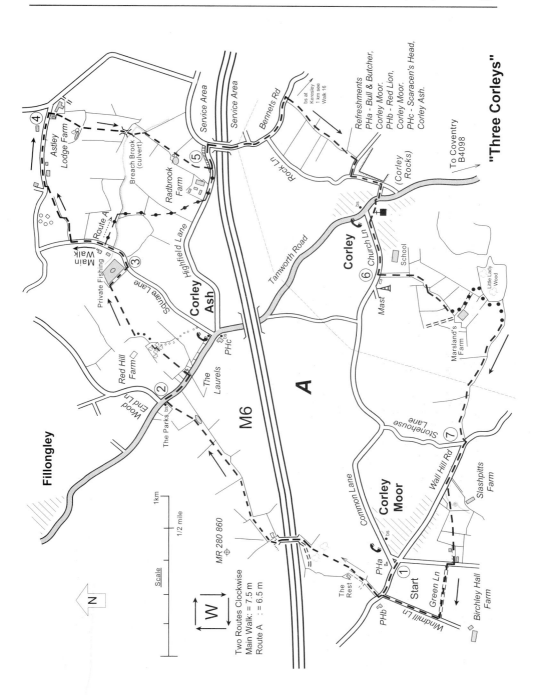

"Three Corleys"

Fillongley

Corley Ash

Corley

Corley Moor

Start

N

W

Scale
1km
1/2 mile

MR 280 860

Two Routes Clockwise
Main Walk: ═ 7.5 m
Route A ∶ ═ 6.5 m

Refreshments
PHa - Bull & Butcher,
Corley Moor.
PHb - Red Lion,
Corley Moor.
PHc - Scaracen's Head,
Corley Ash.

To Coventry
B4098

Astley Lodge Farm

Breach Brook (culvert)

Service Area

Service Area

Bennets Rd

bs at Keresley
1 km see Walk 16

Rock Ln

(Corley Rocks)

Radbrook Farm

Highfield Lane

Route A

Main Walk

Private Fishing

Square Lane

Tamworth Road

Church Ln

School

Little Lady Wood

Mast

Marsland's Farm

Red Hill Farm

The Laurels

Wood End Ln

The Parks bs

PHc

M6

A

Common Lane

Stonehouse Lane

Wall Hill Rd

Slashpitts Farm

PHa

The Rest

PHb

Windmill Ln

Green Ln

Birchley Hall Farm

© Crown Copyright

Start : Junction of Watery Lane & Green Lane, Corley Moor.
Grid Ref. SP 279,850
See page 87 for Allesley start at The White Lion.
Direction : Anticlockwise.
Main Walk: = 8.0 miles
Route A : = 6.0 miles
OS Maps : Landranger 140
: Pathfinder 935
: Explorer 221
Refreshments : (page 100
Bull & Butcher, Corley Moor.
Red Lion, Corley Moor.
White Lion, Allesley.
Pub. Transport : (Page 101
Start 735.
On or near route
West Midlands 900.
Parking : Triangle opposite Bull & Butcher, Corley Moor.
Alternative start White Lion, Allesley. Customers please ask permission.

Snippets:-
Some of the woods date back to the 16th century and earlier. On Route A, north of Elkin Wood, is the source of Bridle Brook, a tributary of Coventry's River Sherbourne. Elkin Wood is one of Coventry's Ancient Woodland Nature Reserves (owned by The Woodland Trust). Was the Tin Tabernacle manufactured by Boulton Paul?

Wildlife

A late summer walk on the edge of the Meriden woodland complex includes some interesting grassland features.

Brief Information and Outline of Route

Traditionally Warwickshire has been divided into two parts; 'Feldon' and 'Arden'. The Feldon country (the field land) lies to the south of the Avon and was traditionally regarded as the more prosperous, intensively farmed region. Arden (the Woodland), in contrast, was a more hilly landscape (in part above the 500 ft contour), with poorer soils and little land under the plough. (Warwickshire CC and Coventry CC have produced landscape and design guidelines to help protect, conserve and reclaim the local character of Arden.)

From Watery Lane in **Corley Moor**, walk along Green Lane left down Windmill Lane right at Birchley Hall Farm to skirt Birchley Hays Wood. Turn left and cross Pickford Brook up to Harvest Hill Lane, before turning left, Marlbrook Hall Farm can be seen with the remains of a moat.

Opposite Ivy House turn right down to Meriden Shafts, so called because of past mining in shallow pits. Turn left on Showell Lane past the old Coventry Water Works, and forward past Alspath Hall on the right, a delightful old farm house.

Cross the fields to go over Pickford Brook again, past Harvest Hill Farm and Whitehouse Farm. Look for the view of Coventry spires from the southern most kissing gate of Alton Hall Farm. Turn right onto Oak Lane to Hawkes End across the River Sherbourne.

Turn left across fields to Piker's Lane, then over fields to Wall Hill Road by the source of the River Sherbourne. Continue past wood on right to then turn left across fields to join Wall Hill Road again. Cross fields by Slashpitts Farm and back to the Mission Church (The Tin Tabernacle) and Green Lane.

Kevin Wilkins

Slashpitts Farm

On reaching Birchley Hays Wood you will discover a young pine plantation (approximately 30 to 40 years old) with an open canopy and a ground flora dominated by bramble. Bluebell, bracken, ferns, foxglove and wood millet also occur with some holly, rowan, birch, oak, hazel, hawthorn and dog rose around the wood's perimeter. A wide and damp woodland ride is visible from the footpath at one point and this contains a wide variety of tussocky grasses and sedges with marsh thistle, figwort, great willowherb, rush and meadow vetchling. This area of conifer plantation gives way to an interesting area of semi-natural oak woodland with ash, birch and some dense area of hazel. Bird life is particularly noted in this wood and it is perhaps worth taking a moment to see what's about. Keep an eye out for buzzards!

As you approach Meriden Shafts you will note that a large part of the woodland has recently been clear felled leaving a small area of broadleaf woodland containing abundant birch with rowan and oak and a stand of young larch plantation. During the spring the area of larch plantation through which the footpath passes contains abundant patches of bluebell but as summer progresses becomes dominated by bracken. Keep an eye open for wood millet, a tall woodland grass, which is quite common in this area.

On exiting the woodland you pass through a couple of fields to the south of Meriden Shafts. These fields are grazed by horses and used in part for horse jumping. The grassland itself is particularly rich and contains species such as devil's bit scabious, betony and meadowsweet. Fragments of semi-natural oak and birch woodland also occur at the perimeter of the grassland and include such species as holly, enchanter's nightshade, wood avens, herb robert and red campion.

On reaching Oak Lane you may wish to take a break and visit one of the smallest nature reserves managed by the Warwickshire Wildlife Trust. This reserve is noted for its population of wild daffodil but also contains yarrow, ribwort plantain, black knapweed, common bird's foot trefoil, black medick, sorrel, bluebells and pignut.

As you head east off Oak Lane you will encounter areas of ridge and furrow, an ancient field pattern, suggesting that the pastures were once used for arable cultivation. The area also contains a small field used for rough grazing containing creeping cinquefoil, bird's foot trefoil and selfheal. The grassland is bordered by a dried up brook dominated by tall aquatic grasses beyond which lies a small area of semi-natural woodland of oak, alder, hazel and ash.

Going north from Wall Hill Lane you will encounter an area of oak and birch woodland on a gentle west facing slope with holly, bluebell and bracken. Some hazel and rowan also occurs.

Elkin Wood Route A

Elkin Wood is a 12 acre ancient bluebell woodland that was purchased by The Woodland Trust in 1997 following a year long fund raising campaign, in partnership with Coventry City Council, Allesley Parish Council and the local community. The woodland is now under the long-term management of The Woodland Trust and is freely open to the public to enjoy.

Junction of Oak, Bridle Brook & Washbrook Lanes - A God Cake

Maureen Harris

Alternative Start from Allesley (*Alleslega* in 1176, woodland clearing of a man called Aelle).

This alternative start gives more options for public transport and joins the route at Note 6. It adds about 1.4 miles to the route. From bus terminus see map to get to Wall Hill Road.

From the White Lion walk up Wall Hill Road. Go thro' 2nd k/g left (300m), just past old city boundary post. **Fwd** cross-field, keep parallel to fence posts on right, past pond on right to p/g, then k/g. **Fwd** to pylon and thro' k/g to lane. **T/L**, after 50m **T/R** onto path, fc-right thro' edge of copse to k/g. **V/R**, via stile & then k/g to cross farm track to go thro' k/g into short path leading to lane. **Fwd** down lane to T-junction, **T/R** up to farm and join walk at Note 6.

Return via same route, or alternatively take Ted Pitts & Hawkes Mill Lanes.

Main Walk

1. Walk down Watery Lane from the triangle for 250m to **T/R** into Green Lane. At the end of this lane **T/L** until a large double metal gate is reached on right. X-stile at side & follow track with fc-right towards wood **T/L** to field corner. Thro' gap into fenced path, **T/R** & follow path, passing stile on left, to its end. X-stile, wood right to field corner, x-stile. Keep wood right thro' hedge gap to WMP. **T/L** cross-field, over f/b, **fwd** cross-field to x-stile & s/b onto road.

2. **T/L** along road to Ivy House on left, just past ruin opposite, **T/R** to x-stile. Hg-left over three fields to x-stile into sunken track. **T/L** for a short distance & then **T/R** into the woods. Walk down thro' woods to x-stile & s/b, then gradually climb two "horse jump" fields. X-stile in hedge left of wooden building, **fwd** hg-left to x-stile onto road (Showell Lane).

3. **T/L** along road & as road turns right **fwd** over cattle grid & along farm road. **V/L** where track leads to farm on right (Alspath Hall Fm). **Fwd** on track to pass pool on left. Shortly x-stile on right, **fwd** by contouring round (same level) cross-field keeping parallel to fence line on far right. X-stile, **fwd** fc-left go down to culvert, **fwd** uphill, leaving fence on left to top of rise. Downhill to "far left" corner. **T/L** over brook (culvert), thro' k/g, **T/R**, hg-right, up for 200m to go thro' k/g on right & over f/b. **T/L**, hg-left over 2 fields via k/gs to enter road at Harvest Hill Farm (**Route A** see below).

4. **T/L** up Oak Lane for 45m & go thro' k/g on right. Hg-right, pass pond on right, through k/g into farm area. Follow round to the left keeping hg/fc-left. Thro' 2 paddocks with hg-left (3k/gs & s/b). Hg-left & after 120m thro' k/g on left. **T/R**, hg-right to pass pond on right. Just past pond **T/R** thro' f/g gap, **T/L** hg-left. Shortly thro' k/g on left, **T/L** & with hg-left go downhill to bottom, bear round left to x-stile onto farm road. Cross over road & x-stile, **T/L** uphill, hg-left to x-stile in top corner, cross-field, barn on left to x-stile opposite. **V/R** to cross field, x-stile & s/b. **H/R** plus cross-field to go thro' f/g in hedge. **V/L** cross-field to x-stile, f/b, **H/L** cross short corner of next field to x-stile onto road.

5. **T/R** along road passing junction with Clay Lane to the junction with Bridle Brook Lane / Washbrook Lane. **Fwd** down farm track (L.A.Swann Animal Feeds in 2007) thro' k/g to shortly go thro' p/g on left opposite barn. Hg-right to field corner, over brook thro' k/g. **V/R** cross-field to f/b over River Sherbourne. Hg-left over small field to k/g between Holly & Ash. Cross-field towards two telegraph poles, go thro' k/g. Hg-right to go thro' k/g into stable yard. **Fwd** across yard into lane.

6. **T/L**, pass stables & house on left to enter field. Hg-right over next 3 fields to road. **T/L** down Pikers Lane for 50m, thro' k/g on right, cross-field to go thro' k/g. **T/R**, hg-right to Wall Hill Road. Thro' k/g opposite, **fwd** cross-field to go thro' k/g. **Fwd** cross-field keeping the incoming hedge on left. Aim for outer hedge corner to go thro' k/g near holly bush. With wood boundary on right continue up narrowing field to go thro' k/g at end. **T/L**, hg-left over four fields to reach road. **T/R** & shortly take left fork to Corley Moor.

7. **Fwd** for approx. 250m along road, thro' second k/g on left (just past Slashpitts Farm). **H/R**, cross-field to go over stream & thro' k/g. **Fwd** cross-two-fields thro' k/gs. Enter enclosed path & go thro' 2 k/gs & x-stile onto road. **T/R** & walk up road to triangle.

Route A At end of Note 3, **T/L** for 20m, **T/L** along enclosed path, thro' k/g, **V/L** cross-field thro' k/g, **fwd** cross-field to pick up outward corner on left. **Fwd**, fc-left to go thro' k/g on left, continue along enclosed path and front garden to road. **T/L** along road for short distance and **T/R** thro' k/g, fc-left to go thro' k/g. With hg-left over five fields thro' k/gs and f/gs. On reaching fc-right **fwd** to outward corner & continue **fwd** cross-field to go thro' k/g. Cross-field to pick up hg-right & thro' k/g onto drive (Hollyberry Hall Farm). **T/R** to road, **T/L** down road to corner, thro' k/g, **fwd** cross-field to left of building, with hg-left, up & round right thro' a series of gates to farm drive. **T/L** opposite farm thro' p/g. **V/L** cross-field to go thro' k/g. Hg-left to go thro' f/g, cross track to k/g (stables left), keep f/c right to go thro' k/g onto road. **T/L** to join main walk at Note 7.

"Ancient Arden"

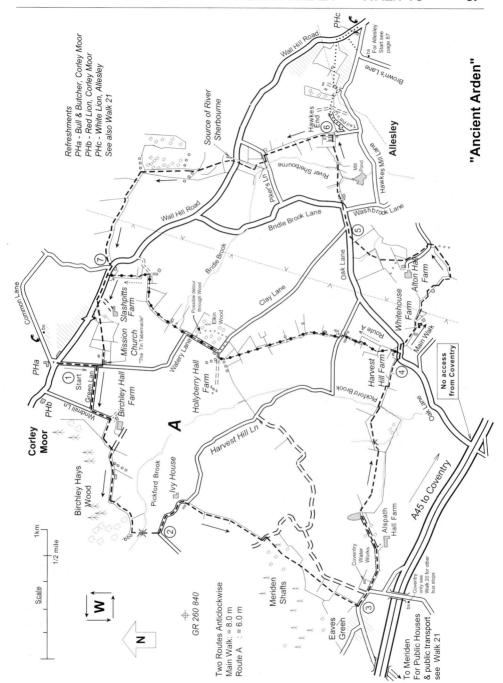

Refreshments
PHa - Bull & Butcher, Corley Moor
PHb - Red Lion, Corley Moor
PHc - White Lion, Allesley
See also Walk 21

Source of River Sherbourne

Wall Hill Road

PHc

For Allesley Start see page 87

Brown's Lane

Allesley

Hawkes End

River Sherbourne

Mill Pond

Hawkes Mill Lane

Piker's Ln

Bridle Brook Lane

Washbrook Lane

Bridle Brook

Oak Lane

Clay Lane

Alton Hall Farm

Whitehouse Farm

Elkin Wood

Possible detour through Wood

Watery Lane

Slashpitts Farm

Mission Church "The Tin Tabernacle"

Birchley Hall Farm

Green Ln

Windmill Ln

Start ①

PHa

PHb

Corley Moor

Common Lane

⑦

Hollyberry Hall Farm

A

Ivy House

②

Pickford Brook

Birchley Hays Wood

Harvest Hill Ln

Harvest Hill Farm

Pickford Brook

Route A

Main Walk

④

No access from Coventry

Oak Lane

A45 to Coventry

Alspath Hall Farm

Coventry Water Works

③

Meriden Shafts

Eaves Green

To Meriden
For Public Houses & public transport see Walk 21

bs Coventry only see Walk 20 for other bus stops

⑤

Scale

1/2 mile 1km

N

W

GR 260 840

Two Routes Anticlockwise
Main Walk := 8.0 m
Route A : = 6.0 m

© Crown Copyright

Start : Old Road, Meriden
Grid Ref. SP 252,820
Direction : Anticlockwise
Main Walk: = 7.5 miles
Route A : = 5.5 miles
OS Maps : (p = part)
: Landranger 139p
: Landranger 140p
: Pathfinder 935
: Explorer 221
Refreshments : ℓ page 100
Queen's Head, Meriden.
Bull's Head, Meriden.
PHs Corley Moor page 82
Pub. Transport : ℓ page 101
Start West Midlands 900.
On or near route 735.
Parking : Carefully in Old
Road or the Queen's Head.
Customers ask permission.

Snippets:- This route uses a
permissive path at High Ash
Farm that enables walkers to
enjoy a continuous traverse
along the west ridge of the
dome at 181m/593 ft. The
late John Smith who charted
all the paths in Meriden
revealed that near the dome is
the source of Pickford Brook,
a waterway that continues to
the Severn. Also the
Hornbrook that passes
underneath Eaves Green
Lane carries on thro' to the
Humber.

Brief Information and Outline of Route

Starting in Meriden (Mereden in 1230, pleasant valley or valley where merry-making takes place) at the Queen's Head, an old coaching inn on the old Holyhead to London Road.

Up Eaves Green Lane to Meriden Shafts, so called because of past mining in shallow pits. Despite this the wood is carpeted with bluebells in spring. Past Ivy House Farm, skirting Birchley Hays Wood, probably a wood for many centuries, to reach Windmill Lane in **Corley Moor**.

Just before the windmill, now a private house, turn left through what looks like the remains of an old orchard. Down past the pools at the back of Old Fillongley Hall, pass Hayes Hall Farm and cross the fields passing the area known as Kinwalsey.

There are stories of the Kinwalsey Elm that stood on the boundaries of Meriden, Fillongley and Hampton from the time when John Wesley and others preached under its branches. Locals called it Kennesy Church. If you would like to locate the old elm, before turning left up Kinwalsey Lane, turn right to the green and sharp bend to see what is left of the elm and the new oak tree planted by the the friends of Meriden Methodist Church in 1984. Apparently, services are still held here in the summer months.

Retrace your steps to rejoin the walk.
Go left up Kinwalsey Lane to the masts, one of the highest points on the walk. Skirt Close Wood and notice the ditch and bank boundary, which is also

Meriden parish boundary. Through Church Wood to High Ash Farm with its wonderful views over Packington Park to the west. Down using a permissive path past Sparrow's Grove to the A45. Cross the bridge and over the fields south to the old A45 and the Queen's Head.

Wildlife

A spring walk which passes through and around a dense collection of semi-natural and plantation woodlands. A real treat for bird lovers and wildlife enthusiast because of its variety of habitats and interesting land topography.

On passing below the A45 along Eaves Green Lane you may wish to take time to examine the hedgerows. These are likely to be several hundred years old and contain hazel, privet, willow, oak, ash, hawthorn, holly and many others besides. Along the base of the hedges and along the road verge woodland ground flora occurs including bluebell, dog's mercury and ferns and suggest that the hedge may have occurred naturally or even be the remaining feature of a woodland that was cleared as part of medieval farming practices.

Having left the road you pass through a couple of fields to the south of Meriden Shafts. These fields are grazed by horses and used in part for horse jumping. The grassland itself is particularly rich and contains species such as devil's bit scabious, betony and meadowsweet which are best seen during late summer. Fragments of semi-natural oak and birch woodland also occur at the perimeter of the grassland and include such species as holly, enchanter's nightshade, wood avens, herb robert and red campion.

A large part of Meriden Shafts has recently been clear felled allowing more light into the area of larch plantation through which the footpath passes. During the spring this wood contains abundant patches of bluebell but as summer progresses becomes dominated by bracken. Before leaving the wood you will pass alongside an area of broadleaf woodland containing abundant birch with rowan and oak. Keep an eye open for a tall woodland grass called wood millet which is quite common in this area.

Birchley Hays Wood includes an interesting area of semi-natural woodland of oak, ash and birch with some dense area of hazel. Bird life is particularly noted in this wood and it is perhaps worth taking a moment to see what's about. Keep an eye out for buzzards!

The walk along Kinwalsey Lane is particularly pleasing. To the west is Close Wood which contains oak and silver birch with abundant hazel and holly. It also contains dog violet, wood sorrel, heath bedstraw, wood avens, herb robert, opposite-leaved golden saxifrage and ferns. Boultbee's Wood is now mainly a pine plantation but worth keeping an eye open for greater spotted woodpecker and tree creepers.

Look out for wood melick along the road verge, which is a grass of limited distribution in Warwickshire, with sweet woodruff and greater stitchwort. Also note the row of small-leaved lime along the woodland bank - a native tree that because of climatic changes is no longer able to set seed and has been able to survive and spread using vegetative reproduction alone.

On leaving the road you will pass by a rich pond containing a host of aquatic and wetland plant species including marsh marigold, yellow iris, lesser spearwort, great bird's foot trefoil, water plantain. The surrounding grassland is also rich with lesser knapweed, betony, sneezewort, perforate St John's-wort, bird's foot trefoil and tormentil. Keep an eye open for amphibians.

The path takes you along the edge of Sparrow Grove, an open canopy oak woodland with frequent birch, hazel and holly. Particularly attractive in the spring with its display of bluebell, although the woodland is dominated by bracken during the summer. The grassland is cattle grazed and contains cat's ear and sorrel with sheep's sorrel, foxglove and hawkbit along the hedge banks. Keep an eye open for buzzard and watch out for amphibia near the pond.

Old Road, an old coach route

Kevin Wilkins

Main Walk

1. With your back to The Queen's Head go left & in a very short distance **T/L** up Eaves Green Lane. Fork right at junction passing under the A45 to reach the junction (Green) at Eaves Green. **Fwd** for 150m along Showell Lane, pass a mobile park then a bungalow on your left, x-stile just inset from the road on left.

2. **Fwd** hg-right, x-stile into a horse field, **fwd** cross-field thro' gap, **V/L** cross-field to go over s/b, x-stile into Meriden Shafts. **Fwd** up thro' woods to the top & x-stile into sunken lane. **T/L** & in 40m x-stile on right into meadow. **Fwd**, hg-right thro' three meadows to reach the road (Harvest Hill Lane) near Ivy House Farm. (**Route A** see below).

3. **T/L** along road, shortly just past house on right x-stile. **V/R** cross-field to go thro' f/g, hg-right down to x-stile. **Fwd** up cross-field to right of railway sheds to x-stile into fenced path adjacent to wood. **T/R** wood on left to end of wood. Thro' gap on left, wood left to corner & **T/R** down track to road. X-stile at side of large double gates. **T/L** down road to just past Hill House.

4. Thro' p/g on left, thro' 2nd p/g then hg-left thro' 3rd p/g. **Fwd** cross-field to to go thro' p/g in left corner (pools left & ahead). **T/R** for a short distance along fenced walkway. **T/L**, fenced pool left, hg-left to x-stile off field corner. **Fwd** hg-left, follow round to right until a large gap. **T/L** thro' gap, initially hg-right, shortly cross-field to large pool ahead (lifebelt) in front of Hall. **Fwd** hg-right up over drive to WMP near field corner ahead. **PLEASE USE PERMISSIVE PATH** (do not attempt to use road). **Fwd**, uphill hg-right to reach field gate to go thro' p/g on left. Continue up with hg-right to exit onto road by stile near top corner. **T/L** for 50m to cross stile on right.

5. **H/L** to climb up behind house to x-stile hidden in corner, **fwd** hg-left, pond on left thro' large gap. **T/R**, hg-right, **fwd** thro' large gap into next field. Initially hg-left, keep **fwd** as hedge veers away to left. Aim for short distance off bottom left field corner (right of large detached house), x-stile & s/b onto road. **T/L** up road (Kinwalsey Lane) & pass between the woods until the end of the wood on your right (Close Wood).

6. X-stile on right into field, keeping wood on right, **fwd** thro' two fields follow round to left. X-stile into wood, **fwd** to x-stile into field with High Ash Farm in view. Cross-field to the farm, cross drive & **fwd** with fc-right to enter another field. **Fwd** with hedge & then wood (Sparrow's Grove) on right to reach & x-stile. **T/R** cross-field & aim for bottom right hand corner of field. X-stile, hg-right, **fwd** to x-stile just off field corner. **H/R**, cross-field, aim for large "old" oak tree, to meet hedge opposite, near the A45. X-stile, cross-short-field, thro' k/g, onto the bank of the dual carriageway. **T/L**, along bank to exit onto Fillongley Road (B4102).

7. **T/R** over A45, just past Meriden sign on left, x-stile right of pair. Hg-left go thro' into second field & shortly **T/L** & **T/R** to follow drainage ditch bank until you are forced right in front of paddock. Follow paddock fence round to right, **T/L** over culvert on left into paddock. Cross-field & thro' k/g onto Old Road, **T/L** to reach The Queen's Head.

Route A At the end of Note 2, **T/L** up the road for 400m. Just before it turns left at road sign x-stile on right over f/b into field, **fwd** cross-field to go over f/b (Pickford Brook), **fwd** until you reach the boundary of Birchley Hayes Wood & WMP. **T/L** along The Heart of England Way with wood on right, **fwd** thro' gap near pool into field. Hg-left to reach road near Hayes Hall Farm. **T/L** for a short distance & continue with Note 5.

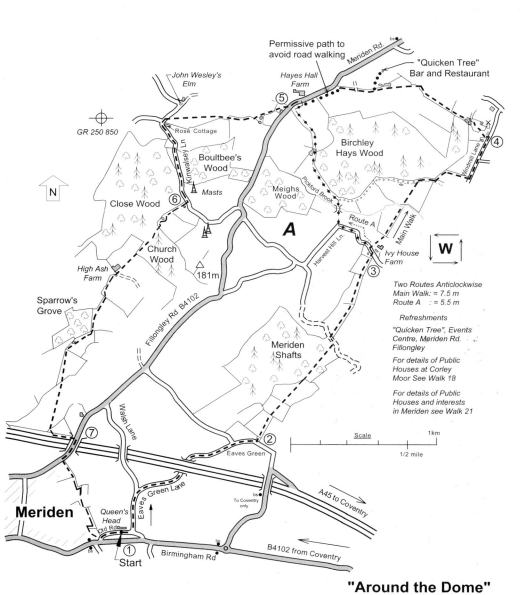

Permissive path to
avoid road walking

"Quicken Tree"
Bar and Restaurant

Meriden Rd.
bs

John Wesley's
Elm

Hayes Hall
Farm

5

GR 250 850

Rose Cottage

Birchley
Hays Wood

4

Windmill Lane

Boultbee's
Wood

N

Masts

Meighs
Wood

Pickford Brook

Close Wood

6

Route A

Main Walk

A

Church
Wood

Harvest Hill Ln.

Ivy House
Farm

High Ash
Farm

181m

3

W

Sparrow's
Grove

Fillongley Rd B4102

Two Routes Anticlockwise
Main Walk: = 7.5 m
Route A   : = 5.5 m

Refreshments

"Quicken Tree", Events
Centre, Meriden Rd.
Fillongley

For details of Public
Houses at Corley
Moor See Walk 18

For details of Public
Houses and interests
in Meriden see Walk 21

Meriden
Shafts

Walsh Lane

7

2

Eaves Green

Scale

1km

1/2 mile

Eaves Green Lane

bs
To Coventry
only

A45 to Coventry

Meriden

Queen's
Head
Old Rd

1

Start

Birmingham Rd

B4102 from Coventry

"Around the Dome"

© Crown Copyright

Start : Queen's Head, Old Road, Meriden.
Grid Ref. SP 252,820
Direction : Anticlockwise
Main Walk: = 4.0 miles
Route A   : = 2.5 miles
OS Maps : (p = part)
         : Landranger 139p
         : Landranger 140p
         : Pathfinder 935
         : Explorer   221
Refreshments : ℓ page 100
Queen's Head, Old Rd
Bull's Head, Main Rd
both in Meriden
Pub. Transport : ℓ page 101
Start West Midlands 900.
On or near route 192 & 194.
Parking : Carefully in Old Road.

Brief Information and Outline of Route

Starting in **Meriden** (see page 90) at The Queen's Head, its oldest inn, built on the original "Old Road" from London to Holyhead. After walking to the north, the main walk descends into the village centre. Here you can stand on the green with the medieval cross, believed by many to denote the centre of England. Also nearby is the National Cyclist's Memorial, commemorating cyclists who died in both World Wars.

Kevin Wilkins

Meriden Village Green

Over the centuries many famous people have visited Meriden. Charles I, hoping to quell Coventry's citizens during the Civil War. Victoria before she became queen, the novelist "George Elliot" and Winston Churchill, who picnicked near Church Lane on his 1945 election campaign.

At the island follow the road towards Hampton in Arden and shortly turn left to skirt the embankment surrounding disused pits and sewage works. Cross The Dowlands and up onto the broad ridge with magnificent views of the Vale of Arden. The late John Smith in his excellent booklet "Meriden Walks" (sadly out of print) pointed out that the Clent Hills and Lickey Hills can usually be seen, as can the heights of Dudley and the Post Office Tower. You can also see aircraft taking off from Elmdon!

After Berry Fields Farm the route eventually joins the line of the original Church Lane, now a footpath. Then into the modern Church Lane and the conservation area of

Snippets:-
The library and information centre can be found by the Green.

A Coventry Way Challenge has been held in the Meriden area since 1998.
Currently, the start and finish are at the village hall.
Previously these were at the Queen's Head public house.

"Alspath", passing the 17th century Church Farm and 18th century old vicarage. Note the old horse mounting stone at the main entrance to the church. Further along on the right is Moat House Farm, part of which dates back to the late 15th century. Traces of the moat can still be seen at the south end of the garden but remember this is in private grounds and not on a Right of Way.

Now turn left through St Laurence's churchyard. The church with its square tower was probably founded in Saxon times. Downhill through kissing gates and back to the Queen's Head. On Route A we pass the following: The Manor Hotel which dates from Tudor times; Meriden Pool that according to legend dries up in times of crisis; Meriden Hall, built in the 18th century and now a Grade 2 listed building; The Bulls Head, another historic coaching inn; Strawberry Bank Hotel, which was originally a farmhouse, then a school during its two hundred year life.

Wildlife

A short walk passing by three ponds. The duck pond opposite the Manor Hotel is typical of this sort of village feature and contains rafts of amphibious bistort within the centre of the pond vying for position over the yellow water lily whilst tussocks of yellow flag iris, weeping willow, alder and white willow line the banks.

Dragonflies, including large hawker species, can be seen during the warmer months demonstrating their flying superiority as they undertake complex aerial acrobatics whilst feeding on flies above the pond.

The churchyard at St Laurence Church is worth a visit; see page 14.

Yellow Flag Iris

A public house goes missing!

Duncan Bean, one of our members from Nottingham, visited Barnacle during one of the annual challenges around A Coventry Way. He had constructed the Association's first web site. Also, as a teenager, he drew the first map for the original A Coventry Way booklet, as well as supporting the first continuous walk round the route in 1974. He was keen to see how the Way had developed so he decided to walk some of the route and enjoy a pint at the Red Lion. To his astonishment the pub had not only closed but he could not find a vestige of its being there.

The closure of village pubs affects us all. They not only rely on custom from the village but visitors from local urban areas as well.

We feel that the constant rural versus urban argument is too negative. We all rely on both communities to support one another and enjoy the facilities and goods that they each offer. Unfortunately, the Union Jack at Stretton on the Fosse, again the only pub in the village, has closed and the building, we are told, has been demolished.

Kevin Wilkins

Queen's Head - Old Road

Main Walk

1. With your back to The Queen's Head go right along pavement of Old Road to near its junction with main road. (**Route A** see below)

2. Go thro' k/g on right, cross-field (paddock) to f/b ahead. **T/R**, ditch right to corner, **T/L** hg-right, then follow up ditch right to meet hedge ahead. **T/L** & shortly **T/R**, hg-right thro' fence gap to x-stile onto road.

3. **T/L** down road on verge & then pavement. **T/L** down Leys Lane, pavement on right, passing pool & Leymere Close on right.

4. 60m after Close **T/R** thro' walkway (Digby Place). Enter cul-de-sac and **T/L** down to junction. **T/L** to main road.

5. **T/R** to Village Green. At the island **T/L** along Hampton Lane using wide verge. After approx 150m **T/L** at The Firs along drive, walkway to x-stile. **T/L** in front of bank for a short distance to exit left onto concrete road. **T/R** down road to corner, **fwd** thro' k/g right of gate into field, **fwd** hedge near left to k/g ahead, **do not go thro'**.

6. With back to k/g **H/L**, aim to pass on your left the end of a brick culvert with two trees a short distance ahead (culverted stream). **Fwd** cross-field up to meet the fence (on your left), **do not cross over the concrete bridge**, use wooden footbridge along the fence to the right. Thro' p/g and **H/R** to cross-short-field corner to go thro' p/g, **H/L**, up cross-field, aiming to pass brickwork and bushes ahead (#), on your left to reach top fence a short distance from top right hand corner.

7. At this point DO NOT EXIT this field. **T/L**, fc-right to go thro' <u>open</u> f/g, shortly **T/R** thro p/g. **T/L**, fc/hg-left **fwd** thro' p/gs & k/g onto road (Berkswell Road).

8. **T/L** for 60m & go thro' k/g on your right, **H/L** to field corner. Thro' k/g & **T/R**, hg-right, thro' k/g **fwd** (ignore gap), hg-right until a second gap (on right) allows you to enter field above.

T/L, hg-left, & follow round to right until reaching a green lane on left. **T/L** down green lane onto road. **Fwd** along road towards the church. Pass old vicarage on your right and church on your left.

9. After the road turns left and just past Moat House Farm, enter church grounds thro' a p/g on left. **H/R** down path to exit into field thro' k/g. Hg-right over next two fields to a small copse that leads you onto Main Road. Cross road to island and over to reach top of steps down to The Queen's Head in Old Road.

Route A

At the end of Note 1, **fwd** to junction, **T/R** along pavement, Main Road. Pass Meriden Hotel and then Manor Hotel on your right, over Leys Lane, Waterfall Close and Glover Close to The Bull's Head. At The Bull's Head cross road. **T/L** for a short distance and **T/R** to enter into the drive to Meriden Hall. After 30m **T/R** along narrow passage over s/b & thro' k/g. Continue with Note 6.

\# From "Meriden Walks" the remains of a bridge over a channel which once carried water from a ram pump back to Meriden Hall.

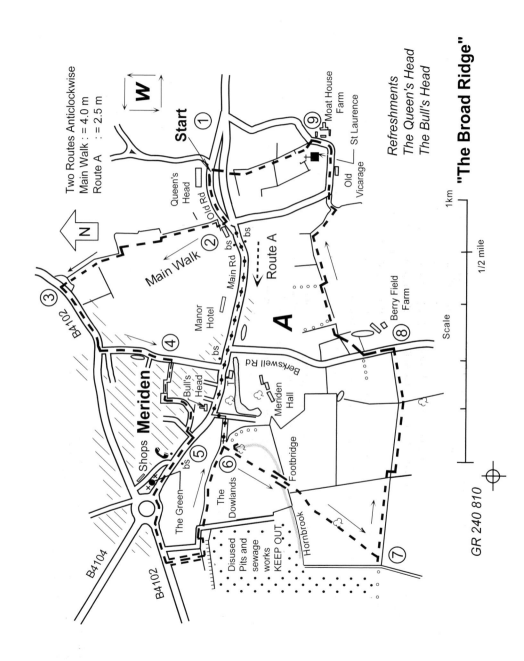

Two Routes Anticlockwise
Main Walk : = 4.0 m
Route A   : = 2.5 m

Start

① ② ③ ④ ⑤ ⑥ ⑦ ⑧ ⑨

Queen's Head

Old Rd

Main Walk

Main Rd

Route A

A

Manor Hotel

Bull's Head

Meriden

Shops

The Green

The Dowlands

Berkswell Rd

Meriden Hall

Footbridge

Hornbrook

Disused Pits and sewage works KEEP OUT

bs

B4102

B4104

B4102

Moat House Farm

St Laurence

Old Vicarage

Berry Field Farm

Refreshments
The Queen's Head
The Bull's Head

"The Broad Ridge"

Scale

1km   1/2 mile

GR 240 810

N   W

© Crown Copyright

Grid Reference Table
All numbers are prefixed SP

The described starting place is at Note 1, alternatives to suit your own travel arrangements can be used.

Walk	Note 1	Note 2	Note 3	Note 4	Note 5	Note 6	Note 7	Note 8	Note 9
1	2738 8029	2749 8135	2632 8121	2508 8163	2542 8050	2555 7951	2603 7968	2660 8004	
2	2448 7758	2475 7815	2460 7916	2577 7780	2563 7683				
3	2724 7665	2691 7559	2559 7579	2621 7614	2563 7683	2578 7778	2644 7798	2695 7714	
4	2803 7206	2913 7263	2970 7321	2901 7474	2841 7548	2691 7559	2620 7428	2670 7306	
5	3221 7730	3103 7696	2968 7504	2970 7352	3198 7350	3283 7258	3382 7533	3394 7576	
6	3283 7258	3316 7215	3345 7141	3294 7123	3325 7274	3235 7261	3247 7280		
7	3631 7223	3611 7106	3588 6935	3459 6870	3458 7001	3335 7135	3513 7176		
8	3631 7223	3771 6984	3977 7066	4058 7244	4029 7322	3862 7444	3795 7398		
9	4123 7562	3860 7447	4028 7322	4107 7272	4296 7279	4316 7424	4213 7499		
10	4164 7583	4391 7465	4486 7583	4490 7716	4462 7796	4374 7909	4296 7720		
11	4029 7955	4130 8078	4257 8020	4301 7909	4293 7770	4160 7766	4126 7662	4052 7733	4040 7906
12	4347 7957	4291 8065	4185 8263	4327 8209	4509 8139	4528 8085	4524 7927	4436 7936	
13	4351 8460	4354 8409	4274 8379	4055 8320	3991 8341	3906 8431	3900 8459	4070 8477	4199 8512
14	3991 8341	3906 8431	3871 8490	3764 8521	3828 8723	3917 8624	4015 8456		
15	3615 8452	3640 8606	3762 8520	3871 8490	3878 8448	3907 8430	3991 8341	3772 8292	
16	2937 8609	2995 8697	3085 8708	3192 8744	3324 8687	3334 8551	3137 8528	3034 8547	
17	2810 8710	2838 8773	2918 8802	2987 8717	2935 8656	2896 8640	2809 8577		
18	2795 8497	2895 8640	2978 8662	3075 8710	3056 8613	2973 8512	2872 8455		
19	2795 8497	2664 8420	2607 8270	2798 8239	2891 8278	2976 8290	2869 8457		
20	2517 8204	2607 8272	2687 8401	2766 8487	2631 8509	2560 8441	2479 8271		
21	2517 8204	2495 8200	2473 8260	2443 8219	2414 8212	2416 8197	2366 8143	2447 8139	2527 8169

Note This table has been updated using GPS data (2007) and will be published on our website, so please let us know if you have more precise GPS data. The GR for the Allesley start, Walk 19, is 3059 8262.

Four figure grid references are given for the beginning of each direction note in Appendix A. For those unfamiliar with grid references the following should get you on your way to understanding them. An excellent free leaflet "Map reading made easy" can be obtained from OS (www.ordnancesurvey.co.uk).

An OS map is covered with squares formed from grid lines, which are spaced 1 km apart.

Eastings are the vertical lines, which increase as you go east. They come first.

Northings are the horizontal lines, which increase as you go north. They come second.

Remember the order by recalling "walk before you climb" = wc.

The bottom left hand corner of each square gives a four figure grid reference, i.e. 2 x two figure, e.g. **55,62**.

For general map purposes six figure grid references are sufficient. To get this third figure imagine the 1 km square divided into ten along each grid line.

This gives squares representing 100m x 100m.

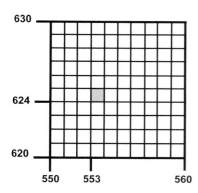

The example on the left shows that the highlighted 100m square is located with a six figure grid reference **553,624**.
This grid reference refers to the **bottom left hand corner** (SW corner). The location is somewhere within this highlighted square.

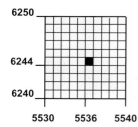

A more precise location can be obtained by using an eight figure grid reference i.e. **5536,6244**.
This position is within the 10m x 10m black square on the left. Again remember that the reference refers to the **bottom left hand corner**. Such references can be obtained by using a GPS instrument, digital mapping, or a compass edge / map card with a 25 000 OS map.

The SP given in front of grid references relates to a specific 100km square in the UK. All of the walks in this booklet are in the SP area.

GPS (Global Positioning System) receivers are becoming cheaper. The old compass will be around for some time; it is lighter and more importantly it does not require batteries. A recent article quoted that "a GPS without a battery is a useless piece of plastic" and that "they eat batteries for breakfast, dinner and tea". However, we have to think of the younger generation being familiar with and wanting to use such gear. Their use on friendly territory, such as the routes described in this booklet, will ensure that when called upon in a more severe environment, their potential and limitations can be better understood. GPS scores when visibility is low, you can find out where you are. But still **don't** leave your compass at home! The first GPS satellite was launched in 1978. There is some uncertainty about the future of the planned European GPS.

Public Houses & Refreshment Outlets

It is strongly recommended to avoid disappointment that you contact your choice to check on whether you can obtain hot food/car parking and confirm opening times.

Village/Location	Name	Telephone	Walk Nos
Alderman's Green	Elephant and Castle	024 7636 4606	15
Allesley	White Lion	024 7633 2841	19
Ansty	Ansty Golf Club	024 7662 1347	13
Ansty	Rose and Castle	024 7661 2822	14,15
Baginton	Old Mill	024 7651 18855	5
Baginton	The Oak	024 7630 1187	5
Berkswell	The Bear Inn	01676 533202	2
Berkswell	Stores/PO/Tea Shop	01676 532279	2
Berkswell Station	The Railway Inn	01676 533284	11
Brandon	Royal Oak	024 7654 2304	11
Bretford	Queen's Head	024 7654 2671	10,11,12
Brinklow	Bull's Head	01788 832355	10,11,12
Brinklow	The Raven	01788 832655	10,11,12
Brinklow	The White Lion	01788 832579	10,11,12
Bubbenhall	Three Horseshoes	024 7630 2108	7
Bubbenhall	Malt Shovel	024 7630 1141	7
Bulkington	Navigation Inn	024 7631 1990	14
Bulkington	Rule and Compass	024 7631 1948	14
Bulkington	White Lion	024 7631 3264	14
Burton Green	Peeping Tom	024 7646 6710	3
Church Lawford	The Old Smithy	024 7654 2333	10
Coombe Country Park	Information Desk	024 7645 3720	11
Corley	Horse and Jockey	024 7633 2643	16
Corley Ash	Saracen's Head	01676 540853	16,17,18,19
Corley Moor	Bull and Butcher	01676 540241	18,19,20
Corley Moor	Red Lion	01676 542345	18,19,20
Cubbington	King's Head	01926 887142	7
Eastern Green	Poacher's Retreat	024 7646 5127	1
Fillongley	Manor House	01676 541369	17
Fillongley	The Quicken Tree	01676 543300	17
Fillongley	Weavers Arms	01676 540399	17
Hawkesbury	The Greyhound Inn	024 7636 3046	15
Kenilworth	Clarendon Arms	01926 852017	4
Kenilworth	Queen and Castle	01926 852661	4
Kenilworth	Abbey Fields	01926 857494	5
Kenpas Highway Coventry	The Burnt Post	024 7669 2671	5
Keresley Village	The Golden Eagle	024 7633 3066	16
Meriden	Bull's Head	01676 523798	1,20,21
Meriden	Queen's Head	01676 522256	1,20,21
Princethorpe	Three Horseshoes	01926 632345	8
Ryton on Dunsmore	Blacksmiths Arms	024 7630 1818	9
Shilton	The Shilton Arms	024 7661 2607	13,14
South Bedworth	Royal Oak	024 76366 477	16
Stivichall	The Festival	024 7684 7921	5
Stoneleigh	Village Club	024 7641 1198	5,6
Stretton on Dunsmore	Oak and Black Dog	024 7654 2416	9
Stretton on Dunsmore	Shoulder of Mutton	024 7654 5525	9
Weston under Wetherley	Bull Inn	01926 632392	7
Withybrook	The Pheasant	01455 220480	13
Wolston	Half Moon	024 7654 2710	9,10,11
Wolston	Red Lion	024 7654 1305	9,10,11
Wolston	Rose and Crown	024 7654 1248	9,10,11

General Notes

When planning your transport for a walk, the Warwickshire Transport Map and Centro Coventry Transport Map and Guide are most useful. Relevant rural bus timetables, leaflets A, E, H, J, K, L & M are available from Warwickshire County Council Transport Publicity Team. The local train services to Tile Hill and Berkswell are suitable for walk Nos 2 and 3.

Important Telephone Numbers

Centro Local Services	024 7655 9559	Bus and train timetable information
Travel Coventry	024 7681 7000	Bus timetable information

Other useful numbers

WCC Transport Publicity Team	01926 412 987	Bus timetables / maps & leaflets

Places where free maps and leaflets etc., can be obtained.

Centro Information Centre Pool Meadow, Coventry
Travel Information Centres
Libraries
Tourist Information Centres
Central Post Offices
and selected rural outlets.

Further Notes

An inclusive day ticket on the first bus will cover other bus and local train journeys within the West Midlands. Although the location of official bus stops are shown, buses will stop, by request, between villages. You may wish to confirm this from the relevant bus company. Telephone numbers can be found on the Warwickshire Transport Map, from timetables or from Centro Hotline. The rural area around Coventry is better served by public transport than generally imagined. For instance, there is a daily half-hourly (including Sundays) service to Birmingham from Coventry passing through Meriden. Also, there are eight buses a day to Brinklow. There are of course services far less frequent. It is considered that, with greater public use and interest, they could be improved. **Walkers are strongly encouraged to use public transport whenever possible, to help protect and recreate a network of safe and pleasant rural routes for walking, cycling, horse riding and quiet recreation.**

Coventry God Cakes.

An extract from CPRE, Warwickshire newsletter. *Most towns or cities have a local delicacy, and the City of Coventry is the place to buy Coventry God-cakes, triangular shaped cakes made by filling inch thick puff pastry with a special kind of mincemeat. They are traditionally served on the first day of New Year, and it is suggested that their shape represents the Holy Trinity. How can grassy islands bear the same name? At present the only explanation is the similarity in their shape - is this too obvious? Grassy islands situated at road junctions always seem to be triangular and apparently formed naturally by the wheels of carts using country lanes. They are fast disappearing from Warwickshire, and we would like to hear from anyone who has knowledge of those that have survived road improvements. The history of our old lanes is little documented and I can find few, if any, references to these delightful islands of grass which are so distinctive at the junction of two or three narrow, winding, obviously old, country lanes. The image of their formation by cart loads of farm produce on the way from field to field, or from farm to market is tempting - could any other reason for their existence be that, because the expense of road maintenance had to be borne by the Parish, any area of road not needing to be kept fit for public use was left untended?*

In preparing the brief information notes, the following publications have been used and wherever possible we have asked permission. Anyone who feels that they have been overlooked please contact the publishers who will ensure that their comments are included in any future revision of this booklet.

We also look forward to any comments or contributions from any walker, villager or interested party that may be used for updating this booklet in the future.

Wildlife Notes by Ian Tanner - former manager of the Habitat Biodiversity Audit (1995-2002), which surveyed and mapped onto GIS the habitats and landscape of Warwickshire, Coventry and Solihull.

Frontispiece Verse by Bill Rogers.

Meriden Walks by John Smith.

Stretton on Dunsmore - The Making of a Warwickshire Village by Stretton Millennium History Group.

Brynca's Low and Brinklow history notes by Diane Lindsay.

Hidden Warwickshire by Betty Smith.

Adrian Dyke and Friends of Canley Ford.

Warwick University's Campus Walks.

Historical notes on Baginton - Gordon Yates.

Historical notes on Stretton on Dunsmore - Denise Hume.

Historical notes on Bubbenhall - Jackie Lloyd of Bubbenhall Parish Council.

Historical notes on Bretford and Brandon - Maureen Harris.

Historical notes on Church Lawford and Kings Newnham - Keith Sinfield.

Warwickshire Industrial Archaeology Society (Pedlar's Bridge).

Warwickshire County Council.

Nuneaton and Bedworth Community Services.

Coventry City Library.

Solihull Metropolitan Borough Council, sketches by Simone Whitehurst (George Kenneth).

A Coventry Way Association members.

Cubbington and Ye Antcent Daies by B M Bean, Cubbington Vicarage 1910.

Coventry City Council, City Development Directorate, Conservation and Landscape Team.

Meriden Centre of England by Doreen Agutter BA.

Coventry Evening Telegraph. Various articles and walking books by Brian Keates.

History of Corley and its Parish Church by The Rev. Ivo Carr-Gregg MA FRCS Vicar of Astley.

Collected Poems and Epigrams by George Rostrevor Hamilton.

Ansty and Shilton by D C D Adams.

Do You Know Coventry by John Ashby.

The Warwickshire Village Book by Warwickshire Federation of Women's Institutes.

100 Years of a Village Under Threat.

Berkswell Miscellaneous by members of the offshoot group of Berskwell Local History Group.

Berkswell Museum.

Warwickshire Landscapes Guidelines - Warwickshire C C / Countryside Commission

Design Guidelines for Development in Ancient Arden - An Historic Landscape Area : Kevin Wilkins and Mike Murray, Coventry City Council, City Development Directorate.

Further reading Brinklow's Story by D E Williams.

Cubbington - Reflections of Village Life, AD1000 - AD2000 by G.F.Peppitt (Pleasuance Press).

Web addresses with associated interests:-

British Waterways	www.britishwaterways.co.uk
Coventry Walks	www.coventry-walks.org.uk
Octavian Droobers	www.octavian-droobers.org
Sphinx Athletic Club	www.sphinxac.org
Massey Ferguson Runners Club	www.masseyrunners.co.uk
Godiva Harriers	www.coventry-godiva-harriers.org.uk

Hedgerows by Ian Tanner (former manager of the Habitat Biodiversity Audit (1995 - 2002)

The history of rural England is imprinted in its landscape and Warwickshire's landscape is defined by its hedgerows. The characteristic of a hedgerow varies with its structure, the field patterns it produces and the plant species contained within each hedgerow length. Even hedgerows that have been removed can leave evidence of past existence. The slightly raised bank within a pasture could have been a hedge line and the mature oak within the arable field may have marked the intersection of hedgerows long since grubbed out.

A correlation between the age of a hedge and the number of species that are contained within a hedge has been established and suggests that hedgerows containing seven or more woody species are likely to be many hundreds of years old. Conversely, a hedge dominated by hawthorn, blackthorn, elder and elm is probably the result of the Enclosures Acts of the eighteenth century.

The Enclosures Acts of that period created what is known as the planned landscape. One can imagine officials with pen and ruler sub-dividing vast areas of unenclosed land on carefully prepared hand-drawn maps. The resulting impact on the landscape will have transformed open expanses of lowland heath and flood plain grassland into a rigid grid of perfectly rectangular fields. In contrast, the more ancient hedgerows often follow the contours of the landscape. Such boundaries may have delineated a Norman Baron's land holding, been the result of slash and burn woodland clearance (to create small areas of pastureland within a forested landscape) or simply arisen along the edge of an ancient trackway.

Footnote - *When on your wanders you may encounter both plant and animal species. Records of such sightings are a valuable source of information to the local record centre, who would be happy to receive any such information. If you can, take with you a note book and field guide, make a note of any features of the species that helped you in your identification, the grid reference of your record, the location, type of habitat, the date. Send your record(s) along with your name, address, phone number to the Warwickshire Biological Record Centre, Warwickshire Museum Field Service, The Butts, Warwick, CV34 4SS.*

Canley Ford Millennium Green by Adrian Dyke, *Canley Ford Millennium Green comprises three hay meadows maintained in the traditional manner, which benefits wild flowers and attracts an array of insects. Over three thousand native trees and shrubs have been planted to supplement the surrounding mature woodland, which is rich in bird life. All three woodpeckers, nuthatches, treecreepers and summer visitors such as blackcaps and chiff-chaffs can be found here. The ancient lane bisecting the site, worn deep by the passage of farm vehicles and animals over hundreds of years, crosses Canley Brook, which is the home of one of our rarest mammals, the water vole. If you are lucky you may catch a glimpse of the kingfisher, and the grey wagtail can often be seen hunting down insects in the ford. The pond is a good place for dragonflies during the summer. Images of the local wildlife have been captured in various works of art, which were installed to stimulate the interests of local children in wildlife and to celebrate the Millennium.* The Millennium Green has been established by Friends of Canley Ford, in partnership with The Countryside Agency, Coventry's Countryside Project, Groundwork Coventry and Warwickshire Wildlife Trust.

Please Follow The Country Code

✔ Guard against all risk of fire.

✔ Fasten all gates.

✔ Help to keep all water clean.

✔ Protect wildlife, plants and trees.

✔ Take your litter home.

✔ Leave livestock, crops and machinery alone.

✔ Keep to public paths across farmland.

✔ Use gates and stiles to cross fences and hedges.

✔ Keep dogs under close control (take special care near animals, particulary on stock farms).

This booklet would not have seen the light of day if the contributors had not given their time voluntarily to preparing and carrying out all the necessary background work. They are listed on this page and pages 4 and 102. Thanks are due to them all. Hopefully, their efforts will be rewarded by the booklet being kept up to date and importantly by more volunteers coming forward to support the local authorities in maintaining all the footpaths and bridleways used in creating the routes. A Coventry Way and its annual Challenge have consumed most of the Association's efforts over the last few years. It now moves forward with the 21 circular link walks that hopefully will encourage more people into that band of countryside surrounding Coventry and acquaint them with the Long Distance Path that is so readily accessible to all.

Committee of A Coventry Way Association 2002 :- Bob Brandon (Chairman), Greta Shields (Secretary), Bob Carey, Bill Day and Bernard Roebuck.
2007 :- John Green (Chairman), Peter Page (Secretary), Bob Carey, John Aylmer (Treasurer)

The audit team co-ordinated by John Green :- Bob Watson, Malcolm & Heather Spencer, Frank Smith, John & Anne Aylmer, Colin Kirkham & family, Mike & Mary Traherne, Jim Davis, Jim Powell, Adrian & Hazel Dyke, Frank Tonkinson, Doug Shelton, Dave Lewis, Stuart Edgwicker, Mos Bailey, Alan Townsend, David & Diane Lathbury, Miranda Aston, Ulli Ull, Bob Rainsley, Phil Lewis, Dave Burrin, Bob & Jo Carey and Paul Drury.
Augmented for 2007 with Bill Hartnett, Bill Eves, Ken Nicholas, Stan Veasey & Peter Page

---

Thanks also to the following for their support :- Bob Watson with his enthusiasm and energy walked all of the routes and estimated the distances. John Aylmer was the first to complete all the walks and submit detailed audit accounts. They were complete and contained humour and encouragement.
Brian Keates and John Hall of the Ramblers' Association for advice and help over many years and their support from the start of this project. Stan Perry for his map and reminiscences.
Bruce Bryant who opened the door to OCAD's demonstration program.
Alan Halliday and Ian Harper at Print5, who provided valuable help and support with printing and publishing queries.
Members from the following clubs :- Octavian Droobers, Sphinx Athletic, Godiva Harriers and Massey Ferguson Runners Club, who offered help and encouragement.
Fred and Ivy Dowell, Keith and Marion Thomas for their encouragement and continued interest over many years.
All of the following from authorities responsible for looking after the Rights of Way have suffered a multiplicity of questions from the Association over the last few years. We thank them for their encouragement and sustained support.
Mike Murray - Coventry City Council; George Kenneth, David Keaney - Solihull Metropolitan B C; Stuart Ikeringill, Geoff Treadwell & Richard Barnard - Warwickshire County Council; Maggie King - Nuneaton and Bedworth B C (Green Track Leaflets are available).

Contact details of authorities responsible for Rights of Way
Any difficulties or if you require advice and are unsure of the area in question please contact :-
Warwickshire County Council on 01926 413427, paths@warwickshire.gov.uk,
www.warwickshire.gov.uk/countryside. If you know the particular authority then use either the above or those shown below :-
Coventry City Council, Coventry's Countryside Project, City Development Directorate, Civic Centre 4, Much Park Street, Coventry, CV1 2PY on 024 7683 1292, mike.murray@coventry.gov.uk
Solihull Metropolitan Borough Council on 0121 704 6429, e-mail dkeaney@solihull.gov.uk
All the authorities produce excellent leaflets and booklets about walking in their areas.
For details use the contact numbers listed.